The Future of the State University

Russell I. Thackrey

THE FUTURE OF THE STATE UNIVERSITY

UNIVERSITY OF ILLINOIS PRESS
Urbana Chicago London

© 1971 by The Board of Trustees of the University of Illinois
Manufactured in the United States of America
Library of Congress Catalog Card No. 79-133944

252 00138 9

To Emily Sheppeard Thackrey
and Ann Thackrey Berry

Foreword

At a time when the rest of the world looks increasingly to American higher education as a model, higher education in the United States is the subject of widespread agitation for fundamental change. There is no substantial consensus as to the nature of the desired changes. Some extremists seek the destruction of the university as an essential precondition to a fundamental, though rarely defined, restructuring of American society. Others seek a variety of reforms, frequently wholly incompatible with each other.

It is almost axiomatic, in higher education circles at least, that one of the great strengths of American higher education lies in its diversity and variety, its control and regulation under state and private rather than federal auspices. At the same time an increasing number of formal study groups, as well as individuals, after stating their strong commitment to preservation of this diversity and variety, proceed to make recommendations as to future responsibility for planning and financing of higher education which seem clearly inconsistent with their initial premise. Also, as the rhetorical public commitment to "universal access to higher education" becomes almost universal—as embodied in resolution after resolution of legislative bodies and citizen groups—the willingness to provide the means necessary to this end appears to recede in inverse proportion to the rhetorical commitment.

It was in this period in our history, at the opening of the decade of the 1970s, that the author was invited by President David D. Henry to give a series of lectures at the Urbana-Champaign campus of the University of Illinois on "The Future of the State University." This book grew out of these lectures. The author had recently retired after 23 years as Executive Director of the National Association of State Universities and Land-Grant Colleges, and was asked to discuss the future of the state university in the context of past developments and present and future trends as he might discern them.

This task was complicated not only by the unpredictable outcome of the current ferment over the future of higher education, but also by uncertainty as to future trends in intergovernmental relations. Will some reasonably stable balance of authority and responsibility between federal and state governments be achieved, or will the rather rapid historical trend toward centralization continue? The implications for higher education are clear.

In the first chapter I have attempted to describe the "state university" as it existed at approximately midcentury, as related to some of the major historical factors in its development to that point.

The second chapter deals broadly with changes since midcentury. Particularly stressed are the impact of the increasing demand for higher education upon state patterns of organization, financing, and coordination; and the effect of vastly increased participation by both the federal government and major private foundations in financing and policy-making in higher education.

The third chapter is a digression, essential to discussion of some of the fundamental issues involved in shaping and determining the future. It is basic to an understanding of one of the most curious phenomena of our times, referred to above: the absence of candor (or perhaps of understanding?) on the part of those currently engaged in making major proposals concerning the future of higher education, in relating the probable future effect of their specific proposals to the generally stated objectives of strengthening higher education while at the same time preserving its diversity and variety of control and support, its freedom from the centralized direction characteristic of higher education in most countries of the world.

The final chapter is necessarily speculative. It is primarily a reflection of the author's concern about some recent trends, and faith and hope for the future.

FOREWORD

This last is conditioned by reflection on the ability of the American people to arrive at wise decisions in the long run, however confused and divided the advice given them, or discouraging the apparent prospect at any one point in history.

The author had the privilege, for nearly a quarter of a century, of working for a remarkable group of men and women holding major administrative posts in the nation's state and land-grant universities. They, and their contemporaries in other higher institutions of the country, have the common fate of occupying what has been correctly described as perhaps the most difficult and demanding positions in American public life, save for the presidency of the United States. There were educational giants among them, but no pygmies; some truly great men in every sense of the word, but no small men. Although I have attempted to give specific credit—in text or footnotes—for specific quotation (direct or paraphrased), these represent only the pinnacle of the mountain of my indebtedness. To acknowledge it fully would require listing scores of names, none of which could be omitted without injustice.

If I have here concentrated on the importance of the history, contributions, problems, future, of the "state university," it is not that I am unmindful of the great importance and contributions of other types of institutions. If I have arbitrarily defined the "state university" at some points as embracing member institutions of the National Association of State Universities and Land-Grant Colleges, it is not that I am unmindful of the stature and significance of many other institutions which share that designation within the several states, but rather for obvious and pragmatic reasons.

Particular personal thanks are due to the administrative officers of the University of Illinois and of its Urbana-Champaign campus, and to the College of Education which provided me with an academic home and the opportunity for informally discussing with graduate students a future which they and their contemporaries will play a major role in shaping.

RUSSELL I. THACKREY
Washington, D.C.

I
The State University at Midcentury
3

II
The State University Today
33

III
Some Basic Issues
58

IV
The State University and the Future
87

Bibliographical Note
135

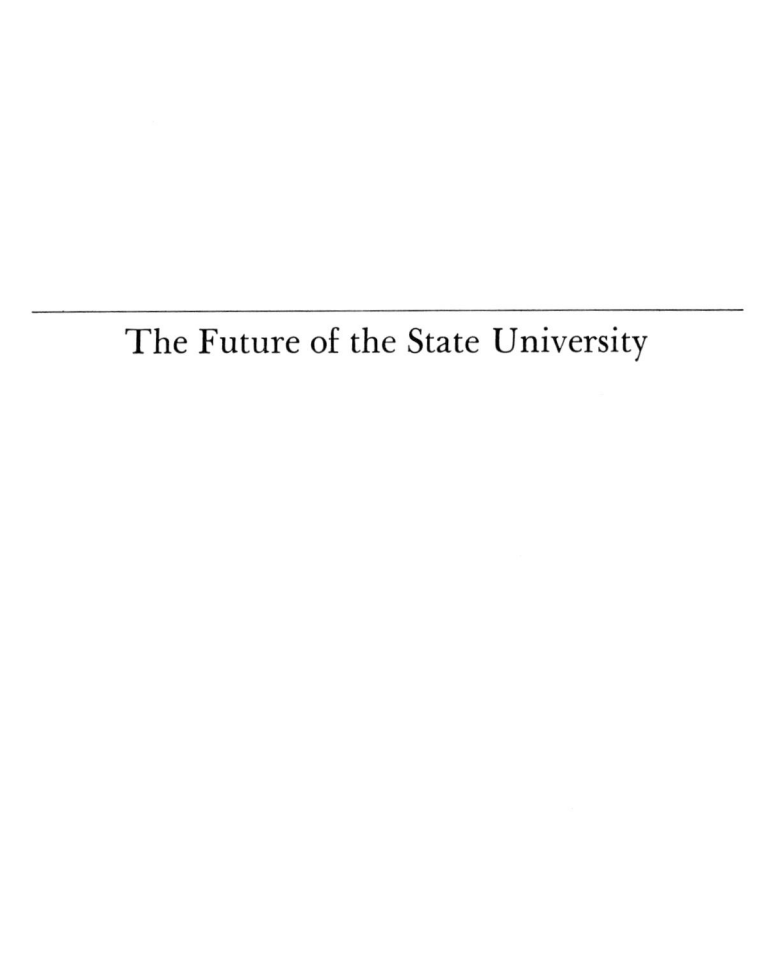

The Future of the State University

I
The State University at Midcentury

If we could first know where we are and whither we are tending, we could then better judge what to do and how to do it.

Abraham Lincoln's comment to the Illinois State Republican Convention in Springfield on June 16, 1858, is a fitting introduction to a discussion of the future of the state university. As an initial point of departure for reflections on the past and present as they affect "whither we are tending" in the future, I have chosen the state university as it had developed at the midpoint of this century, before the impact of a multiplicity of federal programs and the vast and permanent upsurge in the numbers and percentages of young people going to college.

Since the term "university" is now indiscriminately

used to designate a wide range of degree-granting, post–high school institutions, both public and private, some definition of the term "state university" is in order. In this book, the term is in general used as it was in a symposium on the state university at the University of Texas in 1958 as: ". . . a comprehensive state university organized to serve the state as a whole without limitation in function, in scope, or in geographic area."[1]

Having thus defined, it is necessary immediately to qualify. Development of the state university is inextricably associated with the land-grant movement. In more than a third of the states, the designated "land-grant" institution and that early designated as "the state university" are not the same, and in some instances the "land-grant" designation went to a private university. This distinction involves some limitation or sharing of "scope and function." Thus while generalizations are in terms of the fully comprehensive state university, references may be to institutions not fully comprehensive or, indeed, state universities.

Few movements which have so profoundly affected the development of the United States, and indeed of western civilization, have been so neglected by historians as the land-grant and state university movement. To the best of my knowledge, no comprehensive history of the development of the state university exists. As for the Land-Grant Act of 1862, and subsequent related legislation, no acts of Congress have been so

[1] Logan Wilson, ed., *The State University* (Austin: University of Texas Press, 1959), p. 4.

often and admiringly cited and so little studied and understood by legislators, educators, and the public. Two excellent histories of the land-grant movement have been published: one in 1942 dealing with the movement to roughly 1900; and one in 1957 which is comprehensive.[2] Both are now and have for some time been out of print in English, though the second has been reprinted in both French and Spanish because of foreign interest in this great American development. Since land-grant and state universities annually award about two-thirds of this country's doctoral degrees, one may paraphrase Winston Churchill and say "Never have so many written so little about so much."

Historians may in time recognize the fact that the Land-Grant College Act of 1862 may have had more significance than, for example, the Homestead Act or the much larger grants for building transcontinental railroads; or that Justin Smith Morrill and Jonathan Baldwin Turner are more significant figures in American history than some of the relatively obscure men whose biographies adorn current publications lists. Meanwhile, the University of Illinois has made an important contribution through its publication of the record of the first national meeting of land-grant college heads in Chicago in 1871, its republication of the life of Jonathan Baldwin Turner, and its spon-

[2] Earle Dudley Ross, *Democracy's College: The Land-Grant Movement in the Formative Stage* (Ames: Iowa State College Press, 1942). Edward Danforth Eddy, *Colleges for Our Land and Time: The Land-Grant Movement in American Higher Education* (New York: Harper, 1957).

sorship of and publication of Allan Nevins's lectures on the state university.[3]

Painting with a broad brush—but not in the abstract—let us set down some of the distinctive characteristics of the state university as of midcentury. Many of these characteristics were shared with a wide range of other institutions, public and private. This was not always so. Many of the educational reforms either pioneered or advanced by the land-grant state university, and much of its philosophy, have become so widely accepted that other institutions are certain that they must have been first to initiate them.

1. Support by Society, Low or Free Tuition, "Public" Character

The idea that instruction in the state university should be supported by society and open to all, without respect to economic status, is clearly emphasized as a major philosophy of the movement, and explicitly stated in many early state legislative and constitutional pronouncements.

Despite the example of a few states which have a historical tradition of "backwardness" in public higher education, the view that society should as a minimum at least provide instruction and the facili-

---

[3] Richard A. Hatch, ed., *Convention of Friends of Agricultural Education, Chicago, 1871* (Urbana: University of Illinois Press, 1967). Joseph Allan Nevins, *The State University and Democracy* (Urbana: University of Illinois Press, 1962).

ties for instruction had by midcentury been generally accepted as an ideal for public education at all levels, although one frequently not attained in higher education. Indiana's first constitution of 1816, for example, provided that public education from elementary school through the university should be "forever free." Like the camel which first wanted only to get its nose under the tent, fees were initiated in many public institutions as special "laboratory" or other charges, with careful avoidance of the word "tuition" long after students were in fact being required to support general operating costs. But the "public principle" of support, much more basic than the one of technical "control," was at midcentury both widely accepted and not under serious challenge.

2. Comprehensiveness of Scope and Subject Matter

From the beginning the land-grant and state university movement took leadership in broadening the scope of American higher education. Jefferson's earliest writings on the proposed University of Virginia stressed that it would cover virtually all the subject-matter disciplines and professional areas he could envisage at the time, with the exception of theology. Both Virginia and the University of Michigan, frequently called the "mother of state universities," established early models of comprehensiveness which were widely followed. The Land-Grant Act of 1862 was a powerful catalyst, in a variety of ways. It revitalized and broadened the scope of established institutions (some of which were clinging to the narrow list of "traditional" disciplines and professions) and stimulated the founding of a wide range of new institutions. Ezra Cornell envisioned his new "land-grant" university as one which would permit any student to study any subject. Jacob Gould Schurman, third president of Cornell, told a University of Missouri inaugural gathering that a "people's university" must hold all subjects equally reputable and provide instruction in all, with social utilization as the main test. "Greater than the humanities is humanity," he said.

Fortunately for the development of the comprehensive state university, and for all of American higher education, the Morrill Land-Grant College Act, signed into law by President Abraham Lincoln on July 2, 1862, was one of the most beautifully vague pieces of legislation in the history of education, and therein lies much of its greatness.

It authorized the granting of 30,000 acres of public land for each member of Congress from each state, if the state agreed to accept the land and use the proceeds from its sale as a permanent fund for the ". . . endowment, support, and maintenance of at least one college where the leading object shall be, without excluding other scientific and classical studies, and including military tactics, to teach such branches of learning as are related to agriculture and the mechanic arts, in such manner as the legislatures of the States may respectively prescribe, in order to promote the liberal and practical education of the industrial classes in the several pursuits and professions of life."[4]

This broad charter initiated a revolution in higher education and fortunately—in part because it was obviously open to a wide range of interpretation—an affirmative revolution. It did not seek to eliminate or denigrate existing disciplines, or areas of professional emphasis, but to open up higher education to new disciplines, new professions. Jonathan Baldwin Turner had defined the "industrial classes" of the time as 95 per cent of the people, charging that existing colleges served only 5 per cent—the "literary" and leisure classes. He had no objection to serving the 5 per cent in his new universities, if the needs of the 95 per cent were met.[5] The Land-Grant Act of 1862 may be regarded as a broad charter, similar to the U.S. Constitution, emphasizing certain major principles, rather than providing a detailed prescription.

The evidence appears to be that Representative (later Senator) Morrill did not at the time of passage of the act have any clear and specific definition of the terms used in its key paragraph. Fortunately he lived and served in Congress for several decades after passage of the original act and, as a statesman of great stature and the author of the act, was frequently

[4] For text of the 1862 Morrill Act see H. S. Brunner, *Land-Grant Colleges and Universities, 1862–1962*. U.S. Office of Education Bulletin No. 13 (OE-50030) (Washington, D.C.: U.S. Government Printing Office, 1962).

[5] Mary Turner Carriel, *The Life of Jonathan Baldwin Turner* (Urbana: University of Illinois Press, 1961), pp. 68ff.

called on in later years to interpret it. This he almost invariably did in ways to satisfy the friends of broad interpretation.⁶

Could a land-grant institution offer the classics? Of course, said Mr. Morrill, it could not only offer them but had an obligation to do so. Didn't the act say that "other scientific and classical subjects" should not be excluded? This meant, of course, that they must be *included*.

A more controversial question, at the time, was raised by the faculty of the Sheffield Scientific School of Yale University, early designated as the "land-grant" institution of Connecticut. Yale did not have a farm. Was it essential that Yale have a farm in order to carry out the purposes of the act? Could the terms of the act not be satisfied, as Yale was doing, by emphasizing only the education of scientists whose findings might be applicable to "agriculture and the mechanic arts"? Yes, said Mr. Morrill, long after the passage of the act. That was, in fact, the kind of interpretation he had in mind when the act was passed! This interpretation did not please the farmers of Connecticut, who wanted more emphasis on training farmers and led a successful movement to transfer the land-grant designation to Storrs Agricultural College, now the University of Connecticut (with appropriate cash compensation to Yale).⁷ But

---

⁶ See Ross, *op. cit.* I am indebted to Ross and to Eddy, *op. cit.*, for much of the discussion of Morrill and his role in interpretation of the Land-Grant College Act.

⁷ Ross, *op. cit.*, pp. 80–81. There were several other instances in which dissatisfaction with the emphasis of the originally designated land-grant institution led to designation of a different institution or to the founding

it *did* undergird the broad interpretation of the act.

In 1890 Senator Morrill was successful in getting through Congress a second act, providing annual cash grants to the states for the "further endowment" of land-grant institutions, to place them, as the committee report said, on a firm foundation for "so long as we are a nation."[8] This second act, since amended three times to increase the funds available, was considerably more specific than the first in enumerating the purposes for which the funds could be used. No doubt this represented some Congressional dissatisfaction with the emphasis of some institutions. The annual appropriation, said the second act, could be used for instruction in "agriculture, the mechanic arts, the English language, and the various branches of the mathematical, physical, natural, and economic sciences, with special reference to their application in the industries of life."

This second act is sometimes described as an example of federal insistence on narrowly defined categorical or vocational aid. Yet it is difficult to read a highly restrictive purpose or effect into an act which authorized support of instruction, in addition to the broad umbrella of "agriculture and the mechanic arts," in the whole range of mathematics and the

of a new institution. Examples include transfer of designation from Brown to the present University of Rhode Island; from Dartmouth to the present University of New Hampshire; from the University of Mississippi to the present Mississippi State University; from the University of North Carolina at Chapel Hill to the present North Carolina State University at Raleigh.

[8] U.S. Congress, House, *Report 2697*, 51st Cong., 1st sess., 1890. U.S. Congress, Senate, *Report 1028*, 51st Cong., 1st sess., 1890. The two reports are identical, with the exception of additional comments inserted by the House, which accepted the Senate Report.

natural, physical, and economic sciences. This is particularly so in view of later administrative rulings in which the "English language" was interpreted as including language, literature, composition, rhetoric, and oratory, and "economic science" defined as covering "political economy, home economics, commercial geography, and sociology." Mathematical sciences, I would also note, included the whole range of mathematics, plus "book-keeping and astronomy."[9]

As Regent Selim H. Peabody of Illinois said, the Morrill Act "permitted every form of human learning which it has fallen to the fortune of mankind to devise or acquire."[10] It did not provide affirmatively for federal support of every subject matter area, but, as Earle D. Ross of Iowa State University said in his definitive history of the formative phase of the land-grant movement, the wording of the Second Morrill Act marked "an advance in centralized control that paved the way for modern grants-in-aid" and thus was an important precedent, but "the actual restraints laid upon the states were slight."[11]

The stimulus given to the recognition of new professional fields and subject-matter areas by the land-grant act was remarkable. Many of the interpretations of the act which became widely accepted nationally evolved out of discussions and actions of the organization founded in 1887 as the "Association of American Agricultural Colleges and Experiment Stations," the first national association of colleges and uni-

[9] Brunner, *op. cit.*, pp. 63–64.
[10] Ross, *op. cit.*, p. 153.
[11] *Ibid.*, p. 179.

versities and the direct ancestor of the present National Association of State Universities and Land-Grant Colleges. "Agriculture" was from the first broadly defined. Under its wing developed forestry, home economics, and veterinary medicine to a substantial extent. Many present-day schools of business were, I might note, initiated as curricula in "rural commerce." Despite early disputes over the term "mechanic arts," the interpretation as "engineering" quickly prevailed, and enrollments in engineering outstripped those in agriculture in most land-grant institutions (later to be exceeded by enrollments in colleges of arts and sciences, education, and business). The Land-Grant Association settled the argument over "mechanic arts" to its own satisfaction, by adopting a resolution saying that it meant "engineering in all its branches."[12] The first three collegiate schools of architecture in the United States were established at land-grant institutions: Cornell, the University of Illinois, and the Massachusetts Institute of Technology.[13]

3. Democracy in Access to Higher Education: "Open Door Policy"

Access to higher educational opportunity for young people from a wide range of economic, cultural, scholastic, racial, and religious backgrounds was a

[12] Eddy, *op. cit.*, p. 41.
[13] See Chapter IV in *The Architect at Mid-Century: Evolution and Achievement*. Vol. I of the Report of the Commission for the Survey of Education and Registration, American Institute of Architects (New York: Reinhold, 1954).

hallmark of the state university and land-grant movement. If it was an ideal still honored somewhat in the breach with respect to minority racial groups, the state university of 20 years ago still exemplified the ideal more nearly than any other institutional grouping in American higher education.

Let me discuss this topic under three headings:

A. COEDUCATION

The state university was characteristically coeducational, a feature so universally accepted in higher education today as to obscure the long controversy—first over whether women should be admitted to college, and second over whether this should be only in separate but hopefully equal colleges for women. Outside the South, and with some exceptions in the Northeast, most state universities were either coeducational from the beginning or became so in their early history. One source indicates that the Universities of Iowa, Utah, and Washington were among the first to adopt coeducation. In the South, separate colleges for women and men, with the latter frequently organized along military lines, was a prevalent pattern, though by no means the rule. Attitudes toward the "problem" are illustrated in discussions at the historic first national meeting in 1871 of representatives of land-grant institutions. Daniel Coit Gilman, representing the Sheffield Scientific School of Yale said, "We (in the East) are very curious to learn what the experience of the West is in admitting women to the Universities, Colleges, and Schools of Science." Mr. Gilman, later first president of the University of California and Johns Hopkins, said the question of admitting women "has come up this fall . . . at Middlebury and at Amherst College . . . we are all looking with a great deal of interest to the experiences of the West; though none of the New England Colleges have thus far admitted women to the privilege of instruction in any definite way."[14]

President A. S. Welch, of the Iowa State Agricultural College, now Iowa State University and coeducational from the first, argued strongly for coeducation. He said, ". . . the two sexes are of an average quality in their capacity for scholarship. Some of our best students are young ladies. . . . The presence of both sexes, under proper conditions, makes the government less difficult and more wholesome. . . . Sexual isolation for the purpose of culture is contrary to nature; it makes boys rough and girls silly. Of course we have occasional troubles. . . . What college does not?"

President Denison of Kansas Agricultural College (Kansas State University) said some of his regents objected to admitting women, but receded when asked by what right they could be excluded, since the federal endowment "was not given to any particular portion of our citizens." J. M. Gregory of the Illinois Industrial University said women had not been admitted during the first two years "in part because of lack of conveniences for them." Mr. Gregory was inclined to think women should be

[14] Hatch, *op. cit.*, p. 52 and elsewhere, for references in this discussion.

given separate but fully equal colleges of their own but "if you are too poor or too mean to give women equal institutions, then let her be admitted to the best you have. . . ."

He added that, recently, when the regents' committee on admission of women came up with a tie vote, he cast the tie-breaking vote in favor of their admission. He had daughters of his own, he said, and loved them too much to shut the doors of the university to them. (Yale, it may be noted, after studying the "experience of the West" with coeducation for nearly a century, has now gone coeducational!)

B. MINORITY RACES: OPPORTUNITIES FOR NEGROES

Outside the southern and border states, most state universities were open to black students from the beginning. Comparatively few attended. Those that did in many instances suffered from a wide range of discriminatory practices, official and unofficial. Many northern states had comparatively few Negroes in their populations until the great migrations during the depression and the first World War and post-war period (some still do not). Few black families could help finance higher education, and because of prevailing social and occupational discrimination and segregation, many preferred to send their children to the segregated Negro colleges of the South for undergraduate work. Nevertheless, the fact remains that at the undergraduate level, and to a considerably larger extent at the graduate level, the open admissions policies of state universities in two-thirds of the states provided a substantial percentage of the college-educated Negro leadership, including the top administrative officers of many southern institutions.

The legislative, administrative, and judicial branches of the federal government, in my opinion, bear a major share of the responsibility for both the reversal of post-Civil War progress in the area of segregation and discrimination in education in the South, and lack of subsequent progress over many decades. I emphasize this because it is often said that complete federalization of responsibility for many activities is necessary because of a long history of state inaction.

Each of the post-Civil War civil rights amendments to the Constitution, including the fourteenth or "due process" amendment, authorized the Congress to make a law implementing it. The Second Morrill Act of 1890 contained such a provision, possibly the only such provision down to the period of the Civil Rights Act and its successors. It said that the states could not use any of the annual appropriations under the act to support institutions that practiced discrimination because of race. But, it went on to say, if any state established one college for white students and one college for Negro students and divided the money between them "in a just and equitable manner," this would put them in compliance with the antidiscrimination provision.[15] At least four southern states had already made separate Negro colleges beneficiaries of the original Morrill endow-

---

[15] Brunner, *op. cit.*, p. 59, for text of Second Morrill Act.

ment fund. All the other southern and border states proceeded, in due time, to designate or establish such institutions under the stimulus of the 1890 Morrill Act. In 1896 the U.S. Supreme Court, in *Plessy* v. *Ferguson,* laid down the doctrine of "separate but equal," and the sanction of legally enforced segregation (the antithesis of the "freedom of choice" plea now being heard through the land) was complete. Furthermore in the educational institutions the federal government controlled—the public schools of the nation's capital and the military and naval academies—segregation was enforced either by law or in fact for many decades. It was more than 40 years, incidentally, before the federal courts, having posited "separate but equal," began to take an interest in whether separate was in fact equal, which of course it was not and had never been.

Of the nondiscrimination provision of the Second Morrill Act, it may be said that it did provide initial higher educational opportunity for thousands of black students who might not have gotten it otherwise, and that the public Negro institutions were coeducational from the beginning, because legislatures were unwilling to provide separate men's and women's colleges. Until the courts in the 1930s began to look at the "equal" part of "separate but equal," curricular emphasis was largely limited to preparation for the posts open to black college graduates: as teachers in segregated schools, county agents working with Negro families, and (with the aid of scholarships for study outside the state) lawyers, doctors, and dentists serving primarily or exclusively a black clientele.

The effect of federal legal sanction and federal example, of course, permeated the entire country. Yet had all states adopted the policy sanctioned by the Supreme Court, the Congress, and successive Presidents, the United States might today be another South Africa.

As a footnote, one may add that the desegregation of higher education in the South and border states was, with exceptions which can be counted on the fingers of one hand, initiated in almost every state by the public university. In some it was initiated long before the 1954 Supreme Court decision, in some instances by court order in the series of test cases in professional education which preceded the 1954 decision, and in others solely on the initiation of university authorities and with the assent of state authorities. In others it was initiated under court order, and in the face of state laws calling for "closing down" of any institution which violated segregation laws or practices, and under stress of high emotion and physical violence. My point is that, under whatever circumstances it was done, it was the public university which took the lead. Not until the state university had taken the step, and survived, did private colleges and universities follow its example.

C. "OPEN DOOR" ADMISSIONS

The state university at midcentury still in general emphasized the philosophy of "open door" admissions, qualified as it was in many ways and in many institutions and under pressure for further restriction in most. High school graduation was required, except perhaps for a few mature "special students," together with a specific "core" of "college preparatory" subjects, varying with the professional schools. "Open Admissions" did not mean, and had never meant since the early days, that students without extensive exposure to mathematics, for example, could be admitted to an engineering or science course. It did mean that students with subject-matter deficiencies but acceptable records otherwise, might be admitted as "special" or "probationary" students while making up deficiencies. It meant that a student with an "average," or even worse, high school grade record or test score record might be allowed to see whether or not he could meet college standards, if he or she persisted in the face of counseling evidence that the chances were somewhat adverse. And it also meant that within the wide range of curricula offered, the prospective student might, through counseling, find one which best suited his talents and abilities. At the University of Minnesota a study some years ago found that the average academic ranking of entering freshmen in the Arts College and Institute of Technology was equal to that of the most selective private college of the state, while the average of all entering freshmen was approximately that of all colleges in the state. Minnesota, incidentally, offered programs ranging from a two-year terminal "General College" to the doctorate in philosophy in a wide range of fields; and also included two- and four-year terminal technical programs, particularly in the health sciences. At the University of Kansas, also some years ago, a study of an entering class on which high school grades and test scores were available showed that use of "normal" predictors of academic success as a basis for elimination would have denied admission to one-fifth of the graduating class of 1,000 four years later, including one Phi Beta Kappa, several members of the Dean's honor list, and several future engineers, doctors, and scientists. And it would have virtually slaughtered the ranks of those who majored, some with considerable future distinction, in the graphic and performing arts.[16]

The point is that the state university accepted what Dr. C. W. de Kiewiet, then president of the private University of Rochester, described as the "true greatness of American higher education" which is "held aloft on the two pillars of quantity and quality." Dr. de Kiewiet attributed the instability of political and other institutions in many European countries to the academically elitist restrictive practices of their universities. They had failed, he said, "to help in the training of the student of good, but not first-rate ability. . . . The ordinary American graduate, the run-of-the-mine student who would have little chance of being accepted in a British or French university, acquires a literateness in science, an awareness in political and economic issues, a receptiveness in technological affairs, that in the sum total are an incalculable national asset."[17]

Much earlier, William Oxley Thompson, a great

[16] George B. Smith, "Who Would Be Eliminated? A Study of Selective Admission to College," *Kansas Studies in Education* 7, No. 1 (Lawrence: University of Kansas Press, 1956). Reprinted separately, with addendum, 1958.
[17] As quoted by James Lewis Morrill, *The Ongoing State University* (Minneapolis: University of Minnesota Press, 1960), p. 10.

president of Ohio State University, during a celebration of the 50th anniversary of the Morrill Act, reacted strongly against the suggestion that high standards require highly restrictive admissions practices. He said: "The tendency therefore to operate an institution for the sake of maintaining standards is all wrong as I see it. An institution is to be operated for the good it can do, for the people it can serve, for the science it can promote, for the civilization it can advance." Quoting the statement of a New England college president that the function of his institution was to take only "prepared men" and "teach them the essentials," Dr. Thompson said a great contribution of the land-grant state university was to "take unprepared men and make leaders of them."[18]

4. Quality, Standard Setting, Educational Leadership

Founders of state universities almost universally envisioned their institutions as the "capstone" of the state's educational system, providing education of the highest quality and depth. Jefferson's early plan for the University of Virginia called for a system of regional colleges, serving certain counties, with the University at the top of the state's educational pyramid, to which outstanding graduates of the regional colleges would repair for advanced training. This was long before the general development of secondary

[18] William Oxley Thompson, "The Influence of the Morrill Act upon American Higher Education," *Proceedings*, Association of American Agricultural Colleges and Experiment Stations, 26th Annual Convention, 1912.

schools, and Jefferson probably envisioned his regional colleges as their equivalent. Jonathan Baldwin Turner, replying to those who felt all available and limited resources should be put into the public schools before establishment of a university should be considered, used the analogy of a fountain at the summit, its graduates flowing out to nourish all other forms and levels of education. "I never saw water run up hill," he commented. The fact was, of course, that a high percentage of early state universities had to establish their own preparatory schools as "feeders" for the college course.

The ability to maintain high qualitative standards while not practicing elitism in admissions has always been regarded by some critics with considerable skepticism. These critics, however, tend to regard higher education as an intellectual sweepstakes in which all compete for the same prizes and the "winner" takes all. They see the "qualitative" aspect of higher education as one of selecting only those most apt to "win" and enhancing their capacity to do so. Quality in education, however, is properly defined in terms of goals, missions, objectives. The state university at midcentury was a multipurpose institution, serving students with a wide range of talents and educational objectives, through a multiplicity of colleges, schools, departments, each manned by faculties dedicated in common to requiring high standards of achievement. It recognized that each individual has personal goals, that advanced education should not be limited to those who "march to the same drum," or run for the same prize. True, there remained unresolved the hotly debated question of how depth of quality in specific fields and programs—each exploding with new knowledge—could be reconciled with another aspect of "quality"—the responsibility of equipping all graduates with "the common core of knowledge essential to all educated men and women." If this ideal, always to be pursued but never attained, had not been "resolved" in the state university at midcentury, recent advances in sophisticated educational research indicate that the state university's record of performance equaled that of any other category of higher institution. Critics are at last beginning to realize, frequently to their embarrassment, that educational quality is a function of what the university does for the student, and not what the student brings to the university.[19]

My point here, in any event, is that at midcentury it was widely accepted within each state that a first objective in the wise use of public resources available for higher education was to maintain the highest possible level of standards in the state university: not at the expense of quality in other segments of the state's educational system, but as a means of assuring it.

5. Nonsectarianism

The bitter sectarian controversies within the established private colleges were a major factor in the

[19] I refer to the work of Dr. Alexander W. Astin and his associates, who found that much evidence for superior "institutional quality" in higher education is largely the effect of admitting only students with a high predictability of academic success. A report of Dr. Astin's findings appeared in *Science* for August, 1968, pp. 661ff. See also his "Productivity of Undergraduate Institutions," *Science*, April 13, 1962.

movement to establish new and nonsectarian public institutions. Turner, one of that remarkable group of Yale men who contributed so much to the development of both public and private higher education in the "West," was emphatic in his belief that sectarian conflict was incompatible with the development of a true university. Jefferson, in his desire to found a comprehensive university, found himself on the horns of a dilemma with respect to theology. He was bitterly opposed to control of the university by any one sect, yet unwilling to exclude theology as an important and accepted field. He suggested that the problem might be resolved by having theological students take their general college work in the university, and their theological work under the auspices of the various sects and denominations.[20] This idea of the nondenominational, nonsectarian university, publicly supported, with affiliated church colleges or seminaries offering as much or as little instruction under their own auspices and with nonpublic financing as they desire or can afford, has been widely adopted in Canada as a solution—or at least a compromise—on the "church-state" issue.[21] It obtains, in varying degrees of formal and informal relationships, at several U.S. state universities, and appears to be increasingly popular, together with increased emphasis on the offering of nonsectarian programs under university auspices.

[20] See Saul Padover, *The Complete Jefferson* (New York: Duell, Sloan and Pearce, 1943), pp. 957ff., 1076ff.

[21] Geoffrey C. Andrew, "Federal Assistance for Financing Higher Education and Church-State Relationships in Canada," *Proceedings*, Association of State Universities and Land-Grant Colleges, 78th Annual Convention, 1964, pp. 13–18.

6. Dedicated to Research, Advanced Study, the Advancement of Knowledge

The founding of the Johns Hopkins University by Daniel Coit Gilman in 1876 is recognized by educational historians as the first example in the United States of the "true university" devoted primarily to research and the advancement of knowledge. The land-grant movement, however, played a leading and probably the major role in establishment of research as a function of a university in every state and region of the country.

Passage of the Hatch Act in 1887, providing direct federal financial support for agricultural experiment stations, usually at land-grant institutions, was a great stimulus to the development of research, in a climate made favorable by the extensive experience of many leading American educators in German universities. At the time the Hatch Act was passed, half the land-grant institutions already had formally organized agricultural research units, and others were substantially involved in research. As James Grey, University of Minnesota historian, observed: "With the passage of the Hatch Act . . . in the field of agricultural education it became not only legal but obligatory to conduct research. Twenty-five years were to pass before the rest of the university caught up with this view. The Hatch Act may be credited with having launched research in many an American University. . . ."[22]

[22] James Gray, *The University of Minnesota, 1851–1951* (Minneapolis: University of Minnesota Press, 1951), p. 95.

Agricultural research funds supported research in all the biological sciences, in physical science with particular emphasis on chemistry, in many aspects of the social sciences, and in some areas of engineering. The demand for competent research workers greatly stimulated the development of graduate work, in and out of the state universities. Much support was generated for establishing a "National Graduate School" possibly under the auspices of the Smithsonian Institution, a development for a time advocated by the land-grant institutions. In the interim they joined together in sponsoring special summer graduate schools on various campuses, bringing leaders in research together with students. This was followed, or paralleled, by the development of graduate instruction in the larger land-grant, state, and private universities. Interest in a "national" graduate school quickly changed from one of support to one of opposition. Although lack of resources caused graduate work beyond the master's level to be slow to develop in smaller land-grant universities, the stimulus to graduate study of ongoing research, in which students could participate, is clearly evident in the studies of the undergraduate origins of doctoral candidates. Many institutions which have yet to develop major doctoral programs have remarkable "productivity" records of successful doctoral candidates, particularly in the biological sciences. Until World War II, agricultural research was by far the predominant element in continuing federal research support, and its results in application caused the states to much more than match the federal contribution.

7. Public Service to the State and Nation

By the middle of this century, the three functions of instruction, research, and public service were universally accepted by all public universities and by most private universities in this country. Legislation related to the land-grant movement was a powerful stimulus in the development of the "public service" function. The gap between knowledge of good agricultural practices available in the university, and its application on the farm, caused land-grant universities, state departments of agriculture, and the U.S. Department of Agriculture to initiate, more often than not to compete in, efforts to bring research knowledge to the farmer. Businessmen in Texas were persuaded to guarantee farmers against loss if they would try new agricultural practices, and other farmers, suspicious of "book farming," were impressed by the results. County fairs, state fairs, demonstration trains, boys and girls clubs, were used to spread the word. In 1914 the Smith-Lever Act provided federal support for a "cooperative" extension program between the land-grant institutions and the federal Department of Agriculture. The law required evidence of interest and support by farmers, and "farm bureaus" sprang up in every state as sponsors of the cooperative program. These began to hold national meetings and to expand their activities, and thus a great new farm organization was born, much to the unhappiness of other and rival farm groups which began to demand separation of extension and "farm bureau" activities. Each county could get a "county agent" or "farm adviser" by agreeing to contribute to his support, and since problems of the home and family were covered, "home agents" appeared on the scene. The program spread to the cities, where university advisers worked on problems of marketing and, often through the mass media, advised on problems of food purchasing, nutrition, clothing selection; 4-H clubs went with their alumni into the suburbs, and in many cases into the cities.[23]

Stimulated in part by the agricultural example, by the adult education movement in England and the demands of the times, many areas of the university began to move into the field of extension and public service, through classes arranged for the convenience of the employed, correspondence study, lectures, conferences, mass media. Federal support for these activities did not materialize for decades—due in part to rivalries as to what institutions should participate—so the movement grew largely out of limited state support, private gifts, and participant fees. State universities began early to focus attention on problems of state and local government, through municipal reference bureaus, instruction in public administration, special studies of problems of finance and taxation and a whole range of state and municipal problems. There was also a strong consciousness of national responsibility in the state universities. Many

[23] See ". . . A People and a Spirit. Report of the Joint U.S. Department of Agriculture-National Association of State Universities and Land-Grant Colleges Study of the Cooperative Extension Service" (Fort Collins: Printing and Publications Service of Colorado State University, November, 1968).

owed their founding to grants of federal land, either under the Morrill Act or the practice, initiated even before the ratification of the Constitution, of setting aside land in each new territory or state for support of "seminaries of higher learning." Military training —to prepare leaders for the country's defense in time of emergency—was required to be offered by the land-grant institutions, and most at midcentury required participation in the basic course by all male students. So did many other state universities; all offered such instruction, together with a wide range of private institutions. Above all, the state universities recognized that no true university could be parochial in its interest or composition. Students from other states and nations were welcomed. University specialists were heavily involved abroad under the Marshall Plan, and, when President Truman in 1948 advocated extending assistance to the less developed countries of the world, state universities led the response.[24]

8. Public But Autonomous

By midcentury, state universities in general had a high degree of autonomy in the conduct of their affairs, and were in general at least once removed from the arena of partisan political strife. This was accomplished in many states through constitutional

[24] John M. Richardson, Jr., *Partners in Development: An Analysis of A.I.D.-University Relationships, 1956–1966* (East Lansing: Michigan State University Press, 1969). Edward W. Weidner, *The International Programs of American Universities* (East Lansing: Michigan State University Press, 1958).

provision, in others through specific legislation, in others simply through accepted practice. Through the years there had been many exceptions, and there were to be more. But by and large, attempts to involve the university in partisan politics for direct political gain had proved to be both bad politics and bad education. Accrediting agencies stepped in, distinguished scholars went elsewhere or refused to come. Full legal responsibility for the conduct of the university was increasingly centered in boards of trustees usually named by the governor and subject to legislative confirmation. These boards were usually required to be bipartisan, with long enough terms that no one governor could dominate them.

Even when this was not the case, interfering governors were frequently checked by legislative action, and vice-versa. Trustees selected or elected to "straighten out" the university more often than not became defenders, rather than destroyers, of the university. In the long run the public university must be responsive to the society which supports it. In the short run the tradition of autonomy, of separation from the direct line of political executive or legislative controls, allows passions of the moment to die down and the real desire of the people to have a university in which they may take pride to assert itself. As a Colorado court said in a recent case, in which it was asserted that the university was bound by administrative procedures applicable to other agencies of state government, "the university is a unique instrumentality of government." It is not administratively responsible to the governor, but to its own board.[25] A 1959 report of a distinguished study commission on relationships between the state university and state government urged the elimination of many types of purchasing, preauditing and other restrictions imposed by many states on their universities, together with a greater assumption by the university of responsibility for full reporting on and accounting for its expenditures and activities. It was called "The Efficiency of Freedom."[26] The same report urged that states take the initiative in eliminating most or all elected state officials from voting membership on trustee boards, pointing to the inherent conflicts of interest, and partisan issues, that could arise. This plea went unheeded, and time has unfortunately proved the accuracy of the prediction.

The state university at midcentury represented the apex of the state's educational structure. It was comprehensive in subject matter, generous in admission standards but qualitative in its performance requirements, nonsectarian, relatively autonomous, dedicated to instruction, the advancement of knowledge, and public service. Its public character, its distinctive character as a state university, rested primarily on the fact of its support by society.

[25] *Sigma Chi Fraternity* v. *Board of Regents, University of Colorado.* 288 F. Supp. 515 (D.C. Colo. 1966).

[26] *The Efficiency of Freedom. Report of the Committee on Government and Higher Education* (Baltimore: The Johns Hopkins Press, 1959).

II

The State University Today

Of the state university today, as compared to the post–World War II era, it can be said, as Herman B Wells told an audience at the University of Notre Dame: "While the man on the street may have only a dim notion of what the state university was like in the early 1940's, he knows that it has been replaced by something complex and strange. He no longer understands what a university is and does; and he is apt to be fearful of its enlarging influence and rapid growth. Yet he senses that the university is somehow necessary in this complicated world of science-fiction-become-real."[1]

[1] Herman B Wells, "The Growth and Transformation of State Universities in the United States since World War II: The Magnitude and Complexities of the Challenge." Address given at a Conference on the Task of Universities in a Changing World, University of Notre Dame, April 17, 1969. I am indebted to Mr. Wells not only for the quotation cited, but also for other aspects of his perceptive paper.

The state university today as compared to 20 years ago is likely to be much larger, more complex, offer a much wider range of opportunity for disciplinary, or interdisciplinary, specialization; its faculty and student body are more characterized by heavy involvement in graduate work, research, upper division and professional education, all relatively costly in terms of staff, facilities, and equipment.

It is considerably more likely to be a multicampus university, ranging from two or three campuses of comprehensive university character to a "system" involving the whole range of public higher education—community colleges, technical institutes, state colleges, "university" campuses—under one broad administrative umbrella.

Although it is more comprehensive than it once was, it may be in one sense less comprehensive, less clearly the "capstone" of the state's educational systems. Formerly exclusive functions are shared, particularly at the undergraduate level. Teachers' colleges have become multipurpose undergraduate colleges; many have initiated diversified programs of graduate work. New institutions also have been founded. Existing fields of graduate and professional work are sometimes replicated in them or elsewhere and professional fields not previously offered are often located elsewhere than in the "state university."

Major state universities, along with other major universities, have become clearly "national" and even "international" in their graduate, research, and some public service areas, and in financial support. Although state support for higher education has increased phenomenally in absolute terms, it is likely to be relatively less today for the university in terms of "constant dollars per student" (i.e., with adjustments for inflation) and almost certainly so in terms of changing institutional function and emphasis.[2] Fiscal and sheer physical limitations on expansion have brought about limitations on the size of entering classes, in order to care for transfer students from burgeoning community colleges and other colleges into upper division, graduate, and professional work. The numerical "student mix" has shifted from large entering classes tapering down in numbers to the senior class, to what resembles a lopped-off pyramid turned upside down, with the senior class the largest.

Although enrollments in the state university have expanded greatly, they have expanded little if at all in relationship to all other segments of higher education.[3] Enrollments in public higher education have expanded sharply in relationship to private higher education. (Enrollments in private higher education have risen markedly in the past 20 years, but at a considerably lesser rate than in the public sector.) The great relative expansion in numbers in higher education as a whole has come in the compre-

[2] U.S. Department of Health, Education, and Welfare, Office of the Assistant Secretary for Planning and Evaluation, January, 1969. *Toward a Long-Range Plan for Federal Financial Support of Higher Education: A Report to the President.* See pp. 11ff. "The Institutional Financial Picture." (This report is commonly known as the "Rivlin Report" for Dr. Alice M. Rivlin, Assistant Secretary for Planning and Evaluation at the time of its preparation.)

[3] Statement based on personal knowledge of enrollment trends and percentages in "major" state universities as exemplified by membership in the National Association of State Universities and Land-Grant Colleges.

hensive state colleges and community colleges, including many new institutions. Enrollment in the "state university," as traditionally defined, has remained relatively constant as a percentage of all higher education, with a dramatic relative expansion in upper division, professional, and graduate work, and relative decline in the first two years of undergraduate work. Of the 40 or 50 major "universities" in the national sense, today well over half are state universities.

Also pertinent at this point: as relative support from state tax sources declines, students pay an increased proportion of instructional (and sometimes facilities) costs; the ratio of students to "ranked" faculty members has increased; graduate students and teaching assistants, with relatively low stipends, have more responsibility for at least the first two years of undergraduate instruction.

Although the state university today is much stronger in depth and is considerably freer on the whole from certain types of pressures on personal, academic, and other "freedoms," and although the type of gross interference once made possible through such practices as "line item" appropriations, etc., has largely disappeared, it is in other respects clearly less autonomous than it was 20 years ago. Coordinating boards, coordinating-operating boards; advisory boards; even supercoordinating agencies exist in all but a handful of states. A new level of decision-making, or advisory opinion, thus has appeared between the university and its trustees and the governor and the legislature. "Constitutional" universities, held by the courts to have equal legal autonomy with the legislative and judicial branches of government, face the problem of the balance between wise and necessary cooperation in planning and coordination, and legal resistance to gross erosion of their cherished and hard-won status. Long-range university planning and statewide master planning have been generally recognized as essential to the best use of the resources of the university and the commonwealth. In practice this has generally been helpful, but in some instances harmful, and in others useless—the latter when legislatures have rejected recommendations based on extensive study by dedicated and competent individuals. Harmful results have come from failure to appreciate the importance of continuous revision and adjustment, or from the ideological and personal biases which creep into all human efforts. In a few states, traditional arrangements—some with deep historic roots—have been swiftly, perhaps precipitately, abandoned. All education at all levels has been placed under one board, for both policy-making and operations. In others "the state university," sometimes multiunit and with a history of devotion to expansion of opportunity in various areas, has found itself a single-campus unit of a new comprehensive "multicampus state university."[4]

[4] In Rhode Island, for example, public education at all levels has been placed under a single board, replacing separate boards previously responsible for education at elementary-secondary and post–high school levels. In Maine, where separate boards for the University and State Colleges previously existed, a new "University of Maine" has been established under a single board, including all public institutions of higher education. The former multicampus "University of Maine" has become "The University of Maine at Orono." In West Virginia, three boards formerly governing,

My point is here only to emphasize that however desirable—or inevitable—these developments, they impinge on university autonomy in a variety of ways.

The state university of 1970 is both more and less the "people's college" in the many senses of that term, less and more parochial in the composition of its student body, than 20 years ago. It is more truly democratic in its progress toward elimination of a wide range of forms of discrimination: in eligibility for membership in student organizations, in athletics, in housing, in recruitment practices, etc. It typically has a range of affirmative efforts for recruitment of minority students; its curricular offerings reflect minority cultural and other contributions much more extensively and significantly; and its staff, too, shows a significant increase in minority representation. It is under particular difficulties—some shared with its private counterparts, some not—in this effort. With limited staff or physical resources which compel it to exclude large numbers of young people who want to come, it has in the past made its selection by raising "objective" undergraduate admissions standards (test scores, high school grades) to make the student body fit the Procrustean bed. If it now seeks out minority students who can meet its set admissions requirements, it is quite likely to find itself outbid by prestigious private institutions that recruit on a "national" basis and offer full defrayal of all college costs. If it modifies its "set" standards to include

---

respectively, the state's two designated universities and its state colleges, have been replaced by a single board, with a chancellor as chief executive officer. Utah has also abolished various separate boards in favor of a single coordinating-operating board.

other factors indicative of college success, or to include a "high risk" factor, it is likely to incur the wrath of parents whose children were turned down under the "set" standard; or to be charged with "lowering standards," even though performance standards are not involved. And if it recruits qualified minority nonresidents, it is "favoring them over the children of taxpaying residents," a mortal sin. If it attracts qualified scholars from traditionally "black" colleges, it is guilty of the worst possible form of "raiding"; if it does not it will be in serious trouble with civil rights authorities, student groups, and its own "conscience," until the slow process of increasing supply through the graduate schools begins to catch up with demand.[5]

[5] For example, a tuition charge at the University of California was first proposed by state officials on the ground that receipts would be used substantially to finance attendance at the University by students from low-income families, not adequately represented in proportion to such families in the state's population. A survey by the University indicated the situation referred to was due primarily to rigid academic entrance requirements imposed by the "California Master Plan" which restricted university admittance to the upper one-eighth of high school graduating classes. The survey found that 80 per cent of *all students eligible to enter the university* were attending some institution of higher education. To increase enrollment of economically and otherwise disadvantaged students, the University got approval to modify admissions requirements for up to 4 per cent of entering students. While the academic record of those so admitted has been equal to that of those admitted by "normal" criteria, the University has been subsequently charged by some state officials with admitting "unqualified" students whose presence contributes to campus disturbances! See also the remarks of Vice-President Agnew as prepared for delivery in Des Moines, Iowa, on April 13, 1970. As quoted in *The Washington Post* for April 14, 1970, p. A5, the Vice-President took the position that remedial and compensatory programs should be conducted solely by institutions other than "universities"; otherwise "academic standards" will be endangered. This illustrates common public confusion between flexibility in admissions requirements, and in standards of performance required for graduation. The first is amply justified on the basis of experience. The second would, of course, represent a lowering of academic standards.

Although great national, state, and private "student aid" programs have in many ways increased opportunity for the disadvantaged, the steady rise in student charges, accelerated by the drain on normal university resources for "matching" requirements and extensive administrative personnel, has had a countereffect.

The educational and cultural horizons of the state university have greatly expanded. Students and faculty move about more, both within the nation and abroad. Foreign students are present in large numbers. In graduate study, mobility is the prevailing pattern. Faculty "mobility" is commonplace. Yet a strong new force for parochialism is everywhere apparent in public higher education. By legislative fiat, financial necessity, and otherwise, nonresidents face numerical limitations or high boundary fences in the form of sharp fee increases. Even cold figures showing that drying up "normal" and fairly equal "exchange" between adjacent states is costly in terms of drying up income from resident-nonresident fee differentials has had small effect.

It is a commonplace that student alienation in the state university, as in other public and private institutions, large and small, is extensive. Its extent, while not unprecedented, is greater than in the personal memory or experience of those in the university community. It extends, also, to many faculty members, particularly, though by no means exclusively, to younger faculty members and teaching assistants. It is most prevalent among those in the arts, humanities, and social sciences. Many of those involved are highly idealistic, intelligent, disenchanted with many aspects of society as they find it, not career-motivated in the sense of wanting to develop the special competencies for what they view as "establishment" careers in business, industry, science, technology. Idealism is manifest in an unprecedented, and relatively little publicized, willingness to spend long hours working with the disadvantaged or the handicapped, to volunteer for service in the Peace Corps, Vista, etc. A most disturbing aspect is a failure to appreciate that the expertise in science and technology, scorned by many for some of the harmful effects it has produced, is our real hope of correcting the harm that has already been done.

Alienation, of course, has brought confrontation. Most state universities have experienced confrontation, or narrowly escaped it, in a variety of forms, from a variety of motives and causes. In the vast majority of cases it has been nonviolent, or with a degree of violence which would pass unnoticed by the public if it followed a football victory or an outburst of spring dormitory exuberance. In some cases violence has, of course, been severe, recurrent, extreme by university standards, though not by comparison with that occurring elsewhere in our society. Whether the state university has experienced disruptive violence or not, or disruption without violence, the public is likely to think it has, or is likely to have, and wants something done about it. (Not many months ago, the *New York Times Magazine* carried an article vitriolically condemning the activities of students, faculty and administration during disruptions at three major eastern private universities. The author concluded by proposing a "solution": public subsidies to public universities should be cut off and students forced to pay the full cost of their education!) [6]

Concurrently with confrontation there has been an intensification of litigation. Much of this has served the useful purpose of protecting students and faculties from unjustifiable abridgement of their rights, from intimidation; and some has protected university communities from disruption. It also has resulted in prolonged delays in the resolution of pressing problems, in some cases has adversely affected the ability of the university community to act equitably rather than "technically," and has established the major new staff post of university legal counsel in many instances.

Today's state university is more heavily involved than ever in public service, besieged by requests, demands, exhortations that it do much, much more. It may be heavily involved with the inner-city school; with the health problems of and services to the disadvantaged; in technical assistance in trying to solve the problems of environmental pollution; in training for public service; in advising states, municipalities, the national government, on a range of intricate problems; in helping solve the problems of hunger and malnutrition here and abroad. It is unlikely to have more than a fraction of the resources needed to do any of these things. Yet it is not doing enough—can

[6] Irvin Kristol, "A Different Way to Restructure the University," *New York Times Magazine*, Dec. 8, 1969.

never do enough—to satisfy the challenges, hopes, exhortations, which confront it daily.

The state university in 1970, viewed in the perspective of the past 20 years, is in many ways an outstanding example of the capacity of institutions to adjust to changing demands and needs of society. This is contrary to the popular mythology, even among educators. It is contrary to the old joke, repeated whenever administrators get together, that it is harder to get a faculty to change than to move a graveyard. The stereotyped view of resistance and refusal to change is, of course, true of some aspects of the university. But the fact is that particularly in a period of rapid growth, and with new sources of support, the university adapts not only by changing old structures, forms, patterns, but by creation of new structures, by innovation and adoption of the new while preserving the old. If this has an aspect of not lightening the ship by removing the barnacles, I would also note that some of today's proposed innovations represent practices earlier discarded as outworn, and some of today's criticized practices are the innovations which replaced them.

In any event substantial and even drastic change has been widespread, and if much of it is far too little and far too late, it is still well ahead of many institutions of our society.

The field of physical facilities and equipment, perhaps less substantively important than others, will serve as a first illustration. The university community has managed, somehow, to provide facilities, equipment, staff, housing, for a tremendous increase in population with requirements far different in character, complexity and cost than in any earlier period. It is said the national population doubles every 60 years. My own alma mater, probably below the median in this respect, has quadrupled in 30 years, including—on the nonacademic side—provision for a great new and permanent phenomenon, the married student, and major cultural, social, and recreational facilities.

Almost every state university has developed extensive special programs for the "superior" student (although some existed long ago) during the recent but now almost forgotten period when that was the object of special governmental, public, and foundation concern. The growth in depth and range of international programs, and those related to education for international understanding and communication, has been phenomenal. Similar development has occurred in advanced research and education in a wide range of fields and disciplines, some not known 20 years ago.

If the traditional arts curriculum, sometimes called the "four-year lockstep," has sometimes not changed (though it *has* changed considerably in most institutions), new curricula, new roads to the baccalaureate both in time and substance, have appeared. In one recent instance, a student completed all requirements for the baccalaureate in a state university within one calendar year of his matriculation: through intensive summer work, correspondence study, examination.[7] This is an extreme case, but

---

[7] News release from Ohio University, Athens, during 1969.

examination credit, accumulation of both college and high school credit for college work done before high school graduation, waiver of traditional "residence" requirements for mature adults in largely independent study, are common phenomena today. In several instances—some still experimental—students may, after determining their own objectives, virtually write their own curriculums, select their own courses regardless of departmental or college concentration requirements, with assurance of a degree on satisfactory completion. (The safeguard, some would call it the "catch," is that a faculty adviser, or group, must be convinced that the objective is appropriate in educational terms and the "curriculum" relevant to its attainment.) "Pass-fail" grading is also widespread in the undergraduate colleges. It is interesting to note, incidentally, that many of the reforms for which activists are pushing, and policy-makers adopting, in British and continental universities, are in the direction of those long established in the American system, while many advocates of change in this country would reform along European lines.[8]

Adjustments to problems of size, "anonymity of the individual," alienation, lack of "real" student freedom in personal lives or "power" in areas fundamental to students, have occurred in many ways. Parietal rules have disappeared or been so modified as to be unrecognizable by yesterday's alumnus. Students have been given a predominant role, in many in-

[8] Major reforms in higher education in Great Britain as spurred by the report of the Robbins Commission were based in substantial part on a study of American institutions of higher education by the Commission, headed by Lord Robbins.

stances, in making the rules and changing them. Student "living groups" may, and some have, adopted dormitory restrictions far stricter than earlier existed in most universities.

Student representation has appeared on a wide range of departmental, college, and university bodies where it was relatively uncommon before, including university senates and, in a few instances, governing boards. Student governments have acquired a greatly expanded range of authority and responsibility. (In a few instances, student government has been "captured" by activists more interested in demonstrating its futility than exercising responsibility. They have then pushed a broad list of unacceptable, uncompromisable "demands," or declined to exercise judicial functions, forcing faculty and administrative bodies to step in to fill the gap.)

To combat the problems of anonymity and loss of identification, while preserving the real advantages of scale, state universities have responded in many ways. Among them are extensive counseling, guidance, and personnel services. Others include a variety of small semiautonomous colleges—frequently experimental—living-learning dormitories, and scheduling practices designed to put the same students in several of the same classes during the freshman year. Also the office of "ombudsman" has been established at many universities.

State universities today face most serious problems of future resources in areas initiated or developed in depth in response to strong expressions of, and apparent commitments to, "national" or "societal" interest. This is particularly true in the international field, in research and graduate education, in programs to increase opportunities for the minorities and the disadvantaged in general. In each of these areas, in which federal financing and initiative has been heavily involved, recent presidential budgets and ensuing congressional action have resulted in substantial reductions below previous levels of support or refusal to implement (by funding) programs adopted with overwhelming and bipartisan support. (The International Education Act, passed unanimously in one house of Congress and by a lopsided margin in the other, has yet to get its first penny after four years.) Entry to some graduate fellowship programs, and into educational opportunity programs for low-income students, has been cut in half not from authorized but from previous actual levels. All universities, all higher education, are of course affected. Higher education, as represented by degree-granting institutions, clearly has slipped from near the top to near the bottom on the federal totem pole. Major national foundations, also, have sharply shifted their priorities, expressing meanwhile the hope that "other sources" will carry on what they initiated.[9]

The state university today is much more likely to be involved with others in a whole range of coopera-

[9] For example, action of the Ford Foundation in sharply reducing support of the Woodrow Wilson National Fellowship Program was clearly based on expectation of continued expansion of the federal N.D.E.A. Fellowship Program, which instead has been sharply reduced. Foundation support of university international programs has also been reduced in anticipation of increased federal support, but federal support has also since been reduced.

tive arrangements, formal and informal—the former including consortia—than it was 20 years ago. Most of these are designed to make the most efficient use of scarce resources—of talent, library collections, research facilities.

Several arrangements represent efforts, in part, to get over or under barriers to interstate exchange of students. In some areas students are exchanged across state lines, or regional lines, in subject areas not offered in the student's "home" state or institution—sometimes with a waiver of nonresident fees, sometimes involving "full cost" subsidies to the receiving institution. "Developed" institutions assist "developing" institutions and in turn receive substantial reciprocal assistance in many ways. Cooperation between public and private institutions, as such, has greatly increased in many ways. In their "university" aspects in the traditional sense—distinction in research and advanced study—the problems, interests, etc., of major "national" universities are more often than not identical, whether they are "state" or "private" in control. Regional "compacts" or boards in at least three areas of the country cut across all public-private lines. The Education Commission of the States, a national body set up by interstate agreement and covering more than 40 states, involves governors, legislators, educators at all levels. A developing problem on both the regional and national scene is that bodies thus set up to promote cooperation develop tendencies toward "supercoordination" in policy matters.

What are the major forces which have brought

about some of the many changes in the state university since World War II? They are familiar, but a sketchy enumeration of some is useful.

1. The Impact of Developments and Tensions in Our Society

This broad heading I shall use merely to refer to the effect on the university of what may be termed the "revolution of rising hopes and expectations and increasing dissatisfactions." It includes the demand for civil rights and human rights for minorities; the plight of the cities—a direct result of the plight of the dispossessed in the noncities—the constant threat of nuclear destruction; the cold war and the Vietnam war; with all the by-products of the generation gap and the alienation which resulted. These "multiple impacts" are, of course, too fundamentally important to omit, too obvious to need elaboration.

2. The Enrollment Explosion

First among "impacts" was, of course, the tremendous expansion in "demand" for higher education. It came about through a combination of factors: the sharp rise in the birth rate starting about 1940; the growing belief among parents that college education was essential to success in life—however defined—for their children; the increasing tendency to make one or more degrees, or at least substantial post–high school education, a prerequisite for entry into, or advancement in, a wide range of professions and vocations. There followed the change of character and expansion of existing institutions, the founding of new institutions, and the rapid growth of institutions such as community colleges which could be both terminal and also give traditional transfer credit to baccalaureate institutions. These developments impressed legislators, governors, the public, and educators with the necessity to create agencies for broad-scale planning, coordination, assignment of function. Voluntary cooperation among institutions increased substantially, but even the most successful examples were subject to the belief that some new, independent mechanism should be established to assess the results thus arrived at.

3. The Impact of the Federal Government and Foundations

World War II marked the beginning of federal impact on higher education of a scale, complexity, and variety wholly unprecedented. It started with the large-scale involvement of a wide range of university specialists during World War II. It was spurred by the experience of being heavily dependent in areas of basic science on foreign "science" and emigre scientists who fled here from Fascist persecution. It resulted first in the establishment of the National Science Foundation. There followed a fantastic expansion of support for research and advanced training in the health sciences. Then came the Sputnik-spurred National Defense Education Act, with its emphasis on aid to individuals in science and "defense"-

related fields, eventually broadened item by item to include most fields. This was followed by or paralleled by programs of special aid to the disadvantaged, of loans to the relatively affluent faced by sharply rising college costs, and so on. It is not necessary to go further into detail; the important point is that these programs were predominantly, overwhelmingly, categorical or mission-oriented in nature, heavily oriented toward graduate research and education on the basis of individual research proposals, or aid to individuals or categories of individuals to meet sharply rising college charges. Funds were not made available for general operating support of institutions, or for institutionally determined allocation (except under federal specifications). Both the political and bureaucratic popularity of the "categorical" approach, and the long history of stalemate and conflict on educational measures surrounding the "church-state" issue, were among factors reinforcing this trend.

The federal government, in effect, "bought" or supported research for increasingly broadly defined national purposes. It offered specific support for specific projects in federally defined areas, aided individuals, via institutional administrative channels, with loans and grants—usually with substantial contribution of institutional resources.

Any assessment of this effort must weigh the balance heavily on the favorable side. Great advances in contributions to knowledge, in improvement of health, in productive capacity, in educational opportunity, resulted. But it is also a fact that many of the recent trends in higher education which are most criticized today—emphasis on research at the expense of undergraduate instruction; the desire of a wide range of institutions to become "universities" in name and if possible in fact; a loss by many faculty members of an orientation and attachment to the interest and functioning of the university as such, or the problems of the state as such; the alienation of students—are in substantial part the result of lack of balance in federal policies. If federal funds, individual and institutional recognition and "prestige" in national terms, are forthcoming *only* in terms of categorically oriented, research-oriented, individually oriented programs, their effects will not be counterbalanced by lectures by U.S. Commissioners of Education on the importance of undergraduate instruction, or of development of student-faculty-administrative "consensus" on major issues.

The major foundations, with the vast new resources of the Ford Foundation and the lesser but major W. K. Kellogg and Danforth Foundations, added to those of the longer-established Carnegie and Rockefeller Foundations, have played an increasing role in higher education both directly and through their influence on federal policies in higher education. Here, too, an emphasis on international education and graduate education has been followed by a shift to other areas. Through service as members or heads of a variety of Presidential Task Forces and study groups; as federal officials on temporary or long-term leave; through establishment of their own "national" commissions or study groups; the "foundation viewpoint"—to put it loosely—has importantly influenced federal and state policy decisions. Former foundation officials have also become heavily involved, through nonprofit organizations, in major studies and recommendations for federal and other agencies. Again the general result has been beneficial. Yet "foundation philosophy" is usually one of supporting innovation, experimentation, development of new programs, with the expectation that other sources of support will take up the continuing and costly responsibility of carrying on. When government views its role as largely that of "behaving like a foundation," without responsibility for continuing support of programs it has fostered, the effects and implications are much more serious.

In 1952 the report of the Commission on Financing Higher Education was issued. The Commission was a distinguished study group financed by a major foundation and composed and staffed largely by representatives of major private universities. Establishment of this Commission grew largely out of disagreement with recommendations of a 1947 Presidential Commission which urged a vast expansion of federal financing of higher education.[10]

The 1952 Commission: ". . . reached the unanimous conclusion that we as a nation should call a halt to the introduction of new programs of direct Federal aid to colleges and universities. We also believe it undesirable for the Federal government to extend the scope of its scholarship aid to individual

[10] *Higher Education for American Democracy: The Report of the President's Commission on Higher Education* (New York: Harper and Brothers, 1948).

students. . . . Influence flowing from present support is already a cause for concern. Its withdrawal or unwise administration would produce grave results for our institutions. But, in our view, as things are now, such exigencies can be weathered. We are convinced that they would be fatal were Federal support to be substantially extended."[11]

One can smile over the fact that more than half the gross operating budget of some of the institutions represented on that 1952 Commission now comes from federal sources; that the effects are now seen as highly beneficial rather than "fatal"; that the sentiment for maintaining and increasing federal financial support is now as unanimous as was the opposition in 1952. Yet it is equally clear that the prediction of possible "grave results" from withdrawal or unwise administration was sound and is no cause for humor. The issue today is not whether a substantially increased expansion of federal financial involvement in higher education is essential. The issue is now whether or not it can be done without its having "grave results" on a system of higher education which, whatever its faults and in all its diversity, is clearly superior in the quality of its achievement and the democracy of its comprehensiveness to that developed by any other society.

The topic of federal "impact" on higher education calls for a comment on PPB—Program-Planning-Budgeting. In recent years its use has been growing

[11] *The Nature and Needs of Higher Education: The Report of the Commission on Financing Higher Education* (New York: Columbia University Press, 1952).

in all areas of government. Originating in industry and brought into the Department of Defense, it has spread from there to other areas of the federal government largely by "alumni" of the Department of Defense. Program-Planning-Budgeting has had both a useful and a baneful effect. Its admirable rationale is that intelligent decision-making is furthered by the availability of sound information on the probable costs and results of various courses of action. Decision-makers can then choose among a variety of possible goals, or alternative methods of reaching the same goal, with knowledge of the costs and effects of their decisions. Integral to the process, largely conducted by economists, is the availability of reasonably accurate data, in terms of dollars and results. Another factor is that projections must be made over a fairly limited and thus "predictable" time span. Decision-makers in government are under stress to produce "results" in their assured space of office, or as a means of assuring its extension. To a layman such as myself, PPB seems admirably suited, for example, to investments in military hardware, or what is vulgarly termed "getting more bang for a buck." It also makes sense in a wide range of other public policy areas. But it is being widely applied, or attempted, in many other areas in which it doesn't make sense.

Benefits or consequences of the highest social, cultural, and economic importance tend to be excluded from consideration because data are impossible to get, difficult to get, annoying, or don't fit into the directive. For example, one distinguished economist is reported as saying that the economic and social benefits to *society* are undoubtedly great, but until they can be measured in dollar terms, education should be viewed solely as an economic benefit to the individual. (This reminded me of the state auditor in West Virginia, who banned payment of fees to accrediting groups except in the years they visited the university, on the ground that no specific service was performed in the interim.)

Who, for example, can measure dollar value to society of an understanding of the concept of equal justice under the law?

Consider the situation of President Abraham Lincoln in 1862 when the Land-Grant College Act came before him for signature. Latter-day students have called it "the best investment ever made by the Federal government." Frederick Jackson Turner, author of the brilliant analysis, "The Significance of the Frontier in American History," thought the rise of the state university replaced the frontier as the path to opportunity, as guarantor against a closed, hierarchical society based on inherited wealth and social position.

Yet picture Mr. Lincoln, with a Program-Planning-Budgeting staff available to guide his decisions. The country was in the midst of a tragic and costly war. Inflation was rampant, the budget horribly out of balance, and the condition of the Treasury so stark that "printing press" money would soon be issued. The great tangible asset of the federal government was millions of acres of land, land that would predictably rise in price as the war ended and westward expansion resumed. Yet visionaries were asking him to sign a bill to give away millions of acres of land to found colleges of a new and untested character, a bill opposed by the most prestigious educators of the time as an unneeded educational folly. I can hear the PPB voices now:

"Mr. President, we have no basis on which to predict the future economic return from this giveaway, if any. In any event, it will not be during your administration when, hopefully, the war will end and we must return to a sound fiscal footing. Grants for railroads can be justified because they will increase the price of the surrounding land. But for colleges at this time? No, Mr. President. Since prominent members of your party sponsored this legislation, your veto message might suggest that at some time in the future the administration will name a committee of leading educators and businessmen to study this question. You do believe in education of course, but it must wait its turn on the priority list."

Fortunately Mr. Lincoln did not have PPB. The Land-Grant College Act was an act of faith: in the future of the nation, in the young people of the nation. It took 40 years, some say 50, before it clearly began to "pay off," in an agricultural, technological, and cultural revolution on which our emergence as a great nation is substantially based.

III

Some Basic Issues

Having discussed the status of the state university at midcentury and the impact of changes since that time, one more step is necessary before proceeding to a discussion of the future. That is an identification of basic major issues in policy and finance which affect the future of all higher education in this country.

The topics under which I will discuss these issues are (1) the public and private principle in higher education and (2) issues related to the financing of higher education. Who pays for it and how? These topics relate directly to the future of the state university and all other forms of public higher education, and to the future of the private college and university. The issues involved have a direct bearing on the problems of orderly planning and allocation of function in higher education; on the respective roles of students, faculty, administration, and trustees in higher education; on opportunities for minority groups in higher education; indeed to most of the issues of our time related to education.

The Public and Private Principle in Higher Education

It is generally accepted in this country that one of the great strengths of American higher education is the diversity and variety made possible by the existence of strong colleges and universities of both a public and private character. At the same time considerable confusion has existed historically, and exists today, as to the basic distinctions or principles from which this diversity and variety stem.

The U.S. Office of Education, which has the important but technically difficult task of "classifying" colleges and universities under various labels for statistical purposes, has had its problems in the "public-private" area. One major university, for example, has been successively classified by the U.S. Office during the past 25 years first as "private"; then as "public"; and is currently listed as "public-private." This would not be unusual if the institution in question[1] had undergone a major change in its form of governance or methods of financing, but it has not. The changes have merely reflected differing interpretations of the essential distinction between "public" and "private" in higher education.

[1] The Pennsylvania State University.

If the confusion merely involved vexatious problems of orderly statistical classification, it would have no place in a discussion of the future of the public university. But it involves basic policy issues as to the future preservation of what I will term the "public and private principle" in education.

My own interest in attempting to introduce some clarification into the confusion arose with the publication in the summer of 1968[2] of the annual report of Committee Z of the American Association of University Professors, which is concerned with the economic status of the profession. This report focused on the fiscal problems of the private university, its need for substantially increased federal support for operational purposes—including undergraduate education—and the dilemma caused by the fear that direct institutional operating support might result in "governmental control" or "interference" of an objectionable character.

The committee found a solution by suggesting that the basic distinction between the state (public) university and private university is one of "control" and that the private university could remain fully "private" and free from "government control" if funds for general operational support were channeled to the institution through the student—in the form of grants or loans—rather than directly to the institution.

In correspondence with the distinguished chairman of the A.A.U.P. committee, I suggested that the

[2] See Report of Committee Z in *Bulletin of the American Association of University Professors* (Summer, 1968).

essential distinction between the public and private university has far greater ramifications than the technical matter of "control" and that the policy advocated by the committee was therefore based substantially on a false premise. My contention was, and is, that if the policies advocated by the committee in this report became the primary or exclusive method of channeling public funds for the support of higher education, the result would be the substantial elimination of most of the diversity and variety so prized as flowing from distinctions between "public" and "private" endeavor. Major or sole reliance on such a method of financing, I suggested, might be much more likely to invite or be followed by extensive governmental intervention in a highly undesirable form, than a *balance* between this and other methods of financing, including a diversity of sources and methods of support. (I stress the words "balance" and "diversity of methods" in order to make it clear that I by no means advocate that "all" federal funds be allocated directly to the support of institutions of higher education as such, rather than to and through the student. Direct assistance to the economically disadvantaged student is essential now and for the forseeable future, as is the availability of continued direct support of individually initiated research. Exclusive reliance on student aid as a means of making educational opportunity available, however, is to poultice the symptoms rather than cure the disease: the increasing cost-barriers to higher education confronting students and their families.)

My correspondent asked me to state the essential difference between the private and state university. This caused me to reflect on the "public" and "private" principle in education:

THE PUBLIC PRINCIPLE IN EDUCATION

The "public principle" in education is the support by society through general taxation of the provision of educational and related services to the people of that society. Because of this general societal support, the educational services involved should be available to all who are qualified, without respect to race, color, religion, national origin, or other academically irrelevant criteria. Ideally, support by society should be through a tax structure based on ability to pay, and accessibility to all should be on uniform financial terms. Support should be by society as a whole because society as well as the individual benefits. If the individual gains special economic benefits from higher education he will, under an equitable tax system, fully repay, or much more than repay, them during his earning years. Since it is supported by society, the state university is obligated both to be responsible to the needs of society, and to be publicly accountable for the use of tax funds.

Because immediate and direct and partisan political control is inimical to the character of a university, which requires an atmosphere of freedom of intellectual inquiry and expression for its students and faculties, *legal* responsibility for the university has, in nearly all jurisdictions, been placed in a board of trustees, or regents. The powers of this body, its responsibilities, methods of selection, etc., are such as to constitute a unique "instrumentality" of the state. Students of public administration who, in their laudable effort to promote the administrative or legislative efficiency of state government, ignore the unique character of the university and want to lump it administratively and in every other way with, say, the state highway department, do a great disservice to the public interest.

Because the state university is publicly supported, its trustees—or a majority of them—are usually selected by some form of public authority: nomination by the governor and confirmation by the senate is the most common. Other methods include legislative election, direct popular election, ex-officio representation in part, and various combinations of these and other methods.[3]

Although "public control" is one element in the "publicness" of the state university, it is only one element which, if divorced from others, is made relatively meaningless. If, for example, all direct public support were withdrawn from the state university and all funds for its support channeled through individuals, it is difficult to see what essential distinction between a public and private university would remain, regardless of who named the board of trustees. In fact, in at least three, and perhaps more, state universities, a *majority* of the trustees are not named by public sources, yet, because of their public support

[3] E. V. Hollis and S. V. Martorana, *State Boards Responsible for Higher Education,* Bulletin OE-53005, 1960, U.S. Office of Education. (Washington, D.C.: U.S. Government Printing Office, 1960).

and responsibility, it is difficult to distinguish their character from that of other state universities.[4]

THE PRIVATE PRINCIPLE IN EDUCATION

The distinctions between the public and private university are in fact in this country relative and not absolute, but they are important. In its "pure" form the "private principle" in education would be exemplified by an institution which receives no support from public tax sources directly or indirectly. It would therefore be "free" of any public responsibility in any of its practices or programs, except as they violate criminal or civil law. Or, to take a less extreme case, it might (as the U.S. Supreme Court decision said in the Dartmouth College case) be free of state intervention so long as it complied with the conditions of its charter. The Dartmouth College decision said in effect that the state had the right to attach conditions to a public subvention, or in the granting of a charter, but that it could not retroactively void the charter, so long as the specified conditions were being met. The private university in its pure form, exemplifying fully the "private principle" in education, has no "public responsibility," except that which it chooses to assume. It may admit whom it chooses on what grounds it chooses, reject whom it chooses, emphasize what it chooses.

"INDEPENDENCE" IS RELATIVE

A rather widespread custom is to refer to private colleges as "independent" to distinguish them from

[4] University of Alabama, Clemson University, and The Pennsylvania State University are examples.

public colleges. The question is: independent of what? All institutions are subject to the possibilities of pressure from their sources of support, or those responsible for selection of their governing bodies. As an example, one might imagine a private college wholly dependent on a single source of nonpublic funds. To describe such an institution as "independent" is a contradiction in terms. It is independent of public control, wholly dependent on its single source of funds.

The public and private "principles" in higher education are important, and should not be confused. Private support of institutions makes them less vulnerable to the obvious sources of "pressure" or dangers of interference which may accompany the use of public funds. It frequently permits experimentation with initially unpopular or untested programs, or the development of special programs or facilities, which may not be justifiable or feasible through the use of public funds, or the furtherance of religious or social objectives not appropriate for public support. Public support, on the other hand, frees institutions from the open or hidden pressures which may be associated with private funding, or "control." It also permits initiation of programs and experimentation, which may be unpopular with donors or sponsoring bodies. It involves public accountability, responsibility for service to all without discrimination, dedication to the public interest.

Universities are, first of all, universities, and respect common standards of freedom and integrity. The strong, well-endowed private university may by precept and example strengthen the hand of the public university against certain types of pressures. The strong state university may, and does just as frequently, strengthen private higher education against other pressures and temptations.

It is said that the differences between public and private universities are diminishing, and so they are. As private universities seek public and particularly federal support (which they receive in larger relative amounts than public universities), or—as in some areas—state support—they on the one hand *increase* their "independence" of the private sector (by reducing their dependence), and on the other *reduce* it by assuming a public character and becoming dependent on public support. As public universities seek and receive private support for particular programs, they also increase their "independence" and at the same time reduce it, by being responsible for carrying out the purpose for which the particular gift was made.

Diversity and variety of sources and methods of support tend to enrich the quality of universities, and enhance their relative autonomy and integrity. But sound public policy requires that private institutions which receive public support be bound by the same considerations of policy with respect to the use of those funds, and the same degree of accountability, as are public institutions. The reverse, of course, holds true. Public institutions may take on "private" responsibilities through the use of private funds, and private universities discharge "public" responsibilities through the use of public funds. Distinctions may diminish, but it would be an unhappy day if they vanish altogether. The illusion that by channeling all federal funds "through the student" universities can get the money and avoid the threat of federal restriction is just that—an illusion. There is widespread acceptance, in and out of Congress, of the view that it is wrong for government to attempt to control or interfere with universities. But there is very strong legislative and public sentiment to the effect that it is quite appropriate to demand special standards of conduct, and even thought, of individuals who receive federal grants.

The emphasis on the distinction between "public" and "private" in higher education dates roughly from the Dartmouth College decision written by Chief Justice Marshall for the U.S. Supreme Court in 1819.[5] Most early colleges were both founded and aided after founding by a combination of public, private, and—in most instances—church support. Our oldest and greatest private universities were "land-grant" in the sense that they received grants of land from their commonwealths, and other aid from time to time. New Hampshire gave Dartmouth a charter. As time went on, political factions and parties developed, and along with them demands for change in higher education. The president of Dartmouth found his ideas in conflict with those of the Federalist trustees. The governor and legislature, dominated by those of different political persuasion and

[5] For a discussion of the effects of the Dartmouth College case, see Frederick Rudolph, *The American College and University* (New York: Alfred A. Knopf, 1962), pp. 207ff. Elsewhere (pp. 189ff) Rudolph refers to the "myth of the privately endowed independent college" during the early development of American higher education.

educational views, took the side of the president and attempted to take over Dartmouth as a state university and name a new board. The state did, in fact, take such action. Judge Marshall (a Federalist) ruled that New Hampshire, having granted Dartmouth a charter, could not revoke the charter and recapture the gift, so long as Dartmouth operated within the provisions of the charter, which he found it did.

This decision established the principle that the charters and properties of private corporations, including colleges and universities, where relatively immune to revocation or seizure of assets. It served greatly to encourage both the seeking and giving of private support and, until relatively recent years at least, the reluctance on the part of private universities to seek public support.

All institutions of higher education perform, in one sense, a substantial "public service." But the public principle, of tax support by society for the benefit of society, involves specific responsibilities to that society not involved in the case of private support. Similarly private support involves an agreement between giver and recipient as to the use of the funds, which the recipient is bound to respect and which, in general, the civil courts uphold. If we believe that diversity and variety in higher education are good and are advanced by preservation of the "public" and "private" principle, the distinctions should not be allowed to diminish to the point of irrelevance, by stressing technicalities about the importance of "control."

There are a number of instances, particularly in

the Northeast, in which private universities—through contract or other arrangements—perform specific public educational functions, with direct public support. With respect to these functions, they are essentially public with the same responsibilities for accountability, service to the state, nondiscrimination, as the public university, as a series of court decisions is beginning to make clear. Yet they remain essentially "private" in other areas, whose support comes from nonpublic sources. Some of those who advocate channeling support at the undergraduate level primarily through the individual student say this policy would make all universities "publicly supported, but privately independent," and thus create the best of all possible academic worlds.[6] It might as predictably result in the worst of all imaginable academic worlds, a situation in which distinctions between the "public" and "private" principle in education would vanish, with all higher institutions subject to one of the worst forms of interference—being called on to act as enforcement agents for legal restrictions attached to grants to individuals by a centralized legislative authority and wholly lacking either the public or private "independence" that comes from substantial direct public and private support. The integrity and autonomy of the university supported by society are, of course, always dependent on the attitudes of that society toward the importance of protecting that autonomy and integrity. But if society as such is to have no

[6] Dr. Clark Kerr, as quoted in *U.S. News and World Report,* Dec. 30, 1968.

responsibility for supporting and protecting the university, who will?

The Financing of Higher Education

My second topic is certain issues in the financing of higher education. The issues apply to all levels of education, and indeed to all areas involving public support of public services. They are particularly acute, at this time, with respect to higher education.

Who should pay for higher education, society or the individual (with the aid of such family resources as are available) ?

If both, in what proportions, through what channels, and when? Should society help finance the education of all young people, or just some young people: those with "good" cultural backgrounds and high probability of college success? The economically disadvantaged (frequently because of racial or other discrimination)? The middle group in "grademaking" ability and financial resources? All? None? Some? How? When? Through what channels?

The argument that the *individual* should pay "more" or "all" the costs of higher education usually arises in connection with the question of tuition charges, probably because the cost of instruction and providing facilities for instruction has traditionally been regarded as at least in part a social obligation. Indeed it is still commonly accepted as a truism today that "all" or "virtually all" institutions furnish substantial subsidies for the education of their students. This may be true of most institutions if the activities of the whole institution (including research and graduate and professional education) are taken into account. Undergraduate tuition charges, however, have now reached levels in many private institutions at which it seems clear that charges to undergraduates, and particularly to freshmen and sophomores, substantially exceed instructional costs properly allocable to them, with the excess being used to finance much more expensive graduate and professional education, research, and other activities. Indeed, a few institutions, with little or no endowment or other sources of external support, have financed the cost of extensive facilities and the initial development of substantial professional and other programs largely on the basis of student fees.[7]

But the point is that tuition and related charges alone are only a part of the real "cost of higher education." Other costs include those of food and lodging, books and supplies, and the very important element of earnings foregone during the period of college attendance. When these costs are included, it is clear that the student and/or his family pay and always have paid a high percentage of the cost of higher education. Some time ago Dr. Howard Bowen,

[7] Availability of federal support for advanced graduate and professional education and research led many institutions to develop such programs initially—in part—through increased charges to students not in such programs, with the expectation of continued and expanding federal support. With federal support being reduced rather than expanded, such institutions face the problem of curtailing or abandoning such programs—some of great social importance—or requiring students including those not in such programs to support them by paying still higher fees, or by seeking new sources of support. In many instances the states are being called on to "rescue" institutions whose fiscal problems were created substantially by response to federal initiatives, whose promise was not fulfilled.

one of this country's most distinguished economists, estimated this fraction at upwards of 70 per cent.[8] It has no doubt risen since then. If tuition charges were abolished, as they should be, students and their families would still bear a high proportion of the cost of higher education.

The argument for high tuition charges, that is, the argument that students (and their families), or *some* students and their families, should pay virtually all the costs of their education at the time they receive it, is based chiefly on three theories. As stated by Dr. Bowen, they are the "benefit" theory, the "ability" theory, and the "expedience" theory.[9]

The "benefit" theory is that cost of services which benefit individuals should be paid for wholly or primarily by those individuals. Higher education, the argument runs, is primarily of future economic benefit to the student and he (or his family) should pay for it, with neither public support through taxation nor private support through donors being justified. The "ability" argument is that families which can "afford to pay" the full cost of college education should pay it. Therefore, the argument runs, all col-

[8] U.S. Congress, Joint Economic Committee, "Tuition and Student Loans in the Finance of Higher Education," in *The Economics and Financing of Higher Education in the United States*. Prepared by Howard R. Bowen. 91st Cong., 1st sess., 1969. (Washington, D.C.: Government Printing Office, 1969), pp. 618–31.

[9] Howard R. Bowen, "Who Pays the Higher Education Bill?" in *Proceedings: A Symposium on Financing Higher Education, June 12, 1969*. (Atlanta: Southern Regional Education Board, 1969), pp. 3–14. I have also drawn here and elsewhere on a paper, "Finance and the Aims of Higher Education," prepared by Dr. Bowen for a symposium on financing higher education arranged by the American College Testing Service in Washington, D.C., in January, 1970.

lege charges should be set at full costs, with subsidies through tax sources or private donors being available only to students whose families cannot meet those charges.

Under the "benefit" theory in its purest form, societal support from public or private sources would not be involved. Those able to pay college charges would pay them. Those unable to pay would either borrow the money or not go to college. "Market" factors, the willingness of individuals and their families to "buy" or "not buy" higher education, would determine how many individuals went on to higher education, and the nature and the extent of their education.

The "ability to pay" argument admits that wide access to higher education is so important to society that subsidy is justified, but that the subsidy should go only to those who could not otherwise attend college. Therefore *charge* the full costs of education to all, and subsidize the poor so they can pay. The same argument can be made, as Dr. Bowen notes, for a wide range of public services: elementary education, fire protection, public libraries. Its application would call, in these and other areas as well as higher education, either for a system of graduated charges based on income, or individual subsidies based on income. The "ability to pay" theory was widely applied in the early development of the public school system. Free schools or free schooling were, in many areas, legally available only to children of families who took a "pauper's oath" or its equivalent.

As Dr. Bowen notes, the answer to the "ability to pay" philosophy is that "when society wishes to encourage the use of a public service by making it readily available to all, everyone—rich and poor alike—should enjoy that service equally." If the tax system is considered by society as inequitable, bearing relatively more heavily on the poor than on the wealthy, the answer is to reform the tax system. Under an equitably graduated tax system, the well-to-do by no means get a "free ride" when their families use a public service.

The "ability to pay" argument also involves difficulties and costs not normally taken into account by those who advocate it. If college charges are low, hundreds of thousands of students can attend college without special individual subsidy. If they are quite high, the vast majority of students will need such subsidies. Individual decisions as to who gets subsidized and who does not will open or bar the college door. Large numbers of people must be employed to make these judgments, and, particularly if loans as well as grants are involved, to maintain permanent records, act as collection agencies, and so on.

Pressures arise to limit subsidies to the "highly qualified" (i.e., most likely to make good grades), to the "most deserving" (victims of deprivation and discrimination). Not only are extensive financial resources used for administering aid programs, but there is also the very clear risk that many young people who might otherwise attend college will be discouraged by the many difficulties inherent in the process. This applies particularly to those from really disadvantaged backgrounds.

The "expediency" argument for high tuition charges is, of course, just that. It is one of pragmatic "necessity" and is responsible for most of the sharp upward spiral of tuition charges in recent years, particularly in public institutions. As nontuition revenues lag behind due to inflation and increased enrollments, trustees are faced with a variety of hard choices. They include turning away students; reducing quality of instruction by increasing teaching loads; denying salary and wage increases with resultant hardships and loss of able staff; cutting down, postponing, or eliminating new, innovative, and experimental programs (including those of both high social importance and financial cost for the disadvantaged); and raising already high charges with full knowledge that this will "price out" many students unless they are given special aid. The choices may, and frequently do, involve compromise on all these areas, but since there is always an unacceptable limit on cost cutting, tuition charges as the only source of added income go up.

As suggested earlier, despite a truly remarkable increase in state support of public higher education, income per student in public universities as a whole has declined in recent years. In some instances it has gone down even in dollars unadjusted for inflation and, in the vast majority of institutions, down if adjustments are made for inflation and relatively greater enrollments in higher cost upper division, advanced, and professional programs. As a result ratios of students to faculty have increased, and the relative proportion of Ph.D. holders among faculties in public institutions decreased.[10]

It is clear that basing tuition increases on the policy arguments of the "benefit" or "ability to pay" theory are of most questionable validity, while the "expediency" argument is comparable to the choice of a man dying of thirst who finds obviously polluted water. He drinks it as a matter of necessity, not out of a preference for polluted water.

Discussion of *who* should pay for higher education, and in what proportions, proceeds along with, and frequently inextricably enmeshed with, *how* it should be paid for, through what channels. Should all revenues for undergraduate education, for example, be channeled through the student, or "attached to" the student, regardless of their source? Should those for general operational support, facilities, etc., go to the institution directly, as has been the traditional practice in both public and private higher education, but one that is under attack now from various quarters for various reasons? What will be the effects of various policies, or combinations of policies?

If one follows the "personal benefit" theory of higher education financing in its pure form, the answers are simple, though the consequences are rarely

[10] U.S. Department of Health, Education, and Welfare, Office of the Assistant Secretary for Planning and Evaluation, January, 1969, *Toward a Long-Range Plan for Federal Financial Support of Higher Education: A Report to the President.* See pp. 11ff., "The Institutional Financial Picture."

examined. All funds would necessarily come via the student.

However, only a small, though increasingly vocal, number of economists, who appear to have simultaneously discovered Adam Smith and Karl Marx, seriously advocate the "benefit" theory in its pure form. Even most of those who adhere to this general philosophy agree that some form of societal action is necessary to make access to funds for higher education available on a broad scale.[11]

Some would limit this action to making large sums of capital available for loans to those who can't pay. Some would have the federal government, say, furnish the capital for such a loan "bank" (sometimes described glowingly as an Educational Opportunity Bank or Youth Endowment Fund), with borrowings repaid over a long period and collectable by the Internal Revenue Service as a percentage of income received, with such a bank "hopefully" breaking even. Others would rely on more conventional forms of direct government, government-guaranteed, or government-subsidized loans. Again funds would be channeled through the students.

Others see society as having greater responsibility, but would still channel aid through the student: through loans, direct individual grants (usually advocated as limited to those from low-income families), aid for work-study opportunities, etc.

Still others, and I think the vast majority of those

---

[11] See, for example, *Educational Opportunity Bank, a Report of the Panel on Educational Innovation* (Washington, D.C.: Government Printing Office, 1967).

who have thought about the problem, feel strongly first that society should bear the primary responsibility for assuring genuine "opportunity for all" in higher education, and second that the basic method which has made American higher education the envy of and increasingly the model for the rest of the world is sound. That is, through public and private support of colleges and universities as such, enabling them to keep their charges to students low and to offer a wide array of diversity in every imaginable area. They recognize the necessity, even if tuition charges were eliminated, of substantial aids to low-income students for nontuition costs, and provision of borrowing opportunities for others. Given the fact that tuition charges are unlikely to be eliminated, and that wide variations in these charges will continue to exist, they also would support loans, and some forms of direct assistance, to assist student mobility.[12]

Most of these debates and discussions have revolved around federal policy in higher education, but they also are occurring in the several states.

All the discussions, including the one over "channeling funds through the student," are confused by the fact that people carrying them on also have widely differing views and objectives on a whole range of related issues. The words "liberal," "radical," "con-

[12] This is the general position of major institutional-membership organizations in higher education, such as the Association of American Colleges, Association of American Universities, National Association of State Universities and Land-Grant Colleges, the American Association of State Colleges and Universities, the American Association of Junior Colleges, and the American Council on Education.

servative," "moderate," "left," "right," and "middle" hardly make sense in these days as applied to people who may be any one or all of these things with respect to different issues. Nevertheless: "channeling all funds through the student" has a strong appeal to what I would call the "right" or the "radical right" and the "left" or "radical left," and to many in between. From the right one hears the words "individual freedom," "market determination," "play of the free market," "private enterprise," etc., usually associated with support of high tuition charges, the "benefit" theory, and/or the "ability to pay" theory. From the left, one hears "individual freedom" and "freedom of choice" but also, and this is the real key, "student power" as against faculty and administration.

To those who want low taxes, to legislators who dread to raise taxes or unbalance budgets, to some potential benefactors, including foundations, and even to some parents, the idea of shifting the "cost" of education to individual student borrowing or limiting societal support only to low-income students has an obvious appeal. One can salve one's social conscience and still save money. Channeling funds through the students, by loans, grants, or income tax gimmicks, has a strong appeal also to those who want federal money but without federal "control," including those who would like to avoid the First Amendment and the "church-state" issue, or the Fourteenth and the Civil Rights Act. "Free market" economists increasingly assert that education is a commodity which, if bought and sold in the marketplace like any other, will result in the greatest "efficiency" in use of resources. Other forces, other motives, also are at work. Putting higher education fully into the "credit economy" will, as in the case of color television sets, high-powered automobiles, and tropical vacations, open up a vast new source of capital funds to pay higher professorial and other salaries, it is argued. If at the same time public colleges and universities, through operation of the "benefit" or "ability" theories and reduced funding, are forced to raise tuitions sharply, there will be no limit on the extent to which student charges can be raised. All universities would be "private" in their direct reliance on student income, all "public" in the sense of reliance on government to keep the funds flowing.

The argument that a society can, at any given time, shift the cost of education to a future generation (as represented by the student) is, of course, fallacious. The immediate cost is borne by those who furnish the money. If it is government, technical "budget balancing" may be achieved by creation of a special fund or "corporation." But the capital must be furnished and, in order to control inflation, taxes must be increased or federal expenditures for other purposes cut.[13]

[13] Karl Shell and others, "The Educational Opportunity Bank: An Economic Analysis of a Contingent Repayment Loan Program for Higher Education." Working paper, Department of Economics, Massachusetts Institute of Technology, No. 1, November 29, 1967. This paper estimates "fiscal impact" of borrowing for higher education under the proposal as ranging from a minimum of $14 billion to in excess of $20 billion, during the period when repayment of loans would be slight, suggesting that it would be necessary to increase taxes by this amount or cut other public expenditures, in order to control inflation. It is difficult if not impossible to reconcile this with assertions by the sponsors that other forms of federal education aid would not be affected.

In the long run, however, if revenues from college borrowing are channeled back into more loans for new generations of students, the effect is to create a situation in which education is financed, in effect, by a special tax falling only on those who have previously attended college, and borrowed money for that purpose. All others, including those whose parents were affluent enough to make borrowing unnecessary, would escape taxation, to the extent this method was used. Corporations that rely heavily on college talent, individuals of whatever income and whatever background, so long as they either did not go to college or did not borrow for college, *would not be taxed.* Young people looking ahead to a choice of career and forced to borrow from the government "bank" for college would be highly influenced toward occupations promising the highest and quickest financial rewards, rather than the greatest opportunities for career satisfaction, or public service.

In April of 1967 Professor J. K. Galbraith of Harvard told an audience at the University of California, Berkeley: "One of these days, without doubt, some one will urge that universities be put on a profit-making basis with all student accounts handled through the Diners' Club. None of this is a proper subject of complaint. A university must accord liberty even to those who would destroy it, or place its assets in the hands of the sheriff. But while we must accord freedom to damaging nonsense, we must never be passive about it. . . ." (Within five months after Dr. Galbraith made this observation, a press conference was held in Washington, D.C., to unveil a proposal called the "Educational Opportunity Bank." Under it universities would charge all the market would bear, less affluent students would borrow from a federally sponsored corporation to meet the charges, and the Internal Revenue Service rather than the Diners' Club would be the collection agency.)

Proposals to channel all funds through the student do have a certain appeal, if one believes that the question of the relative influence or "power" of students, faculty, administration, and trustees should be settled by giving the entire "power of the purse" to students. It is interesting to contemplate the plight of a college wholly financed by student fees, faced with a mass fee-strike until professor "X" was fired, or if fired, reemployed. Despite my respect for the great contribution students can, should, and do make in the formulation of university policies, I am not impressed by the argument for turning over the future of higher education fully to them on a "consumer's choice" or "the customer is always right" basis. Generally speaking, the concentration of power in any one group or agency, whatever it may be, carries inherent dangers to academic freedom and to the integrity and autonomy of the institution. For this reason colleges and universities have sought a diversity of sources of income.

The possibilities of a reasonable degree of planning and coordination to assure wise use of resources, it seems to me, would be destroyed by the proposal to channel all financial support through the student. How does a state *plan* for the allocation of resources, of functions and programs to institutions, or anything else, in such a situation? If society through taxation furnishes a substantial portion of the resources for higher education, there is an accompanying and inescapable responsibility for some form of societal responsibility for the wise use of those resources. If public tax resources are *not* involved, and higher education is a commodity to be bought and sold like television sets, wash powders, or women's dresses, then not only is educational planning out the window, but some other interesting possibilities arise.

If my television set quickly goes bad, I can at least call on the seller to repair it, sue him if necessary, complain to the Better Business Bureau. Will our colleges of the future be required to guarantee "Financial Success in Ten Years or Your Money Back?" If I pay $20,000 for my higher education and my high school classmate pays $10,000 for his someplace else, will I be entitled to heavy damages if in ten years he is making $50,000 a year in the stock market and I am getting only $10,000 in teaching? And whom do I sue? Will the fashions in higher education change as they do in handbags, with clearance sales of old-model degrees for half the price in half the time?

What happens to our policies of eliminating segregation and discrimination if all funds are channeled through students on a "freedom of choice" basis? The theory of course is that students would "freely" choose the institution they wish to attend, but the other part is that institutions would be "free to choose" the students they admit. This of course is a linguistic and legal absurdity. Students are not in fact free to attend colleges that won't admit them, or colleges to force students to come against their will. Society can require institutions supported directly by the public to eliminate discrimination on irrelevant grounds, such as race, religion, color, national origin. Are we now to use public money to subsidize discrimination and segregation, under the "freedom of choice" theory, which has been struck down by the courts as unconstitutional in the many states which have employed it as a device to subsidize segregation at the elementary and secondary level?

Decisions as to who pays for education, when, how, through what channels, are the key element in deciding the future structure, pattern, extent of accessibility—the important questions affecting the future of higher education in this country. It was the late Senator Robert A. Taft, now regarded by many as the very symbol of conservatism, who once told a group of educators that if the belief that society should directly support such services as the public schools, fire and police departments, libraries, and public parks made him a socialist, then he was glad to accept the title.[14] If many things are best left to free enterprise and the play of the market, education is not one of them, and it is passing strange that higher education should be the subject of extensive agitation for a shift to personal purchase as a commodity, and from institutional to consumer support. One reason may be

---

[14] Robert A. Taft, "Education in the Congress," *The Educational Record* 30, No. 1 (July 1, 1949): 337-56. The reference is to the published text of a speech given by Senator Taft to the annual meeting of the American Council on Education on May 4, 1949. The exact language I have cited does not appear in the published text, which was from a transcript subject to editorial revision on behalf of the Senator, prior to publication. The quotation is from memory and is, I believe, accurate.

that educators have far overemphasized its fiscal benefits, as opposed to its cultural, scientific, political, economic, and social (in the best sense of the term) benefits to our society as a whole. We cannot preach to our young people about their responsibilities for public service, for good citizenship, for placing the welfare of society above narrow and selfish interests, and at the same time tell them that if they want higher education they must "buy" it as the golden key to personal affluence, a hedge against inflation, or a symbol of individual elitism similar to that of having the biggest car on the block. The ideals of a society are embodied in, transmitted through, advanced by, its institutions. As William Oxley Thompson said, a university should exist ". . . for the good it can do; for the people it can serve; for the science it can promote; for the civilization it can advance."[15]

I have referred to federal loans and grants as methods of assisting individual students, or channeling funds for higher education through the student, but not to the various proposals for large-scale financing of higher education through devices related to the income tax. Tax exemption, deduction from gross taxable income for charitable or educational gifts or the support of students, have long been features of U.S. tax policy. They involve problems of equity and public policy which are very real, but have worked well from a pragmatic standpoint and are not likely to be markedly altered in the foreseeable future. More recently considerable sentiment has been aroused for use of the income tax as a major

[15] As quoted by James L. Morrill, *The Ongoing State University* (Minneapolis: University of Minnesota Press, 1960), p. 9.

means of financing higher education, through tax credits related to the amount of tuition or other required college charges other than for board and room. The motivation is that by the "credit" device —withholding money from the Treasury by millions of individuals rather than having it appropriated from tax revenues—the money becomes "private" rather than "public" and thus free from either public policy considerations or constitutional restrictions on the use of public funds. Such proposals are fiscally irresponsible, highly discriminatory against low-income families in that they encourage escalation of college charges without corresponding tax relief, and clearly involve evasion of the basic protections of the Constitution with respect to public policy, by bypassing them. True, they involve a form of societal support of education, but to the primary benefit of those who need it least, and to the detriment, both financially and in terms of discrimination, of those already most disadvantaged.[16]

Decisions as to who finances higher education, and through what channels, are the future determinants of a multitude of basic issues in national and state policy, among them the preservation of the public and private "principles" in higher education, and the extent to which genuine equality of educational opportunity will be realized.

[16] See comments by Chairman Wilbur Mills of the House Ways and Means Committee, *Congressional Record,* Dec. 13, 1967. Also Gerald M. Brannon, Acting Director, Office of Tax Analysis, U.S. Treasury, in "The Tax Credit for Tuition and Fees of Higher Education," a paper presented to the Symposium on Taxation and Education, American Alumni Council, Warrenton, Va., Feb. 8, 1966.

IV
The State University and the Future

In a book that was a bestseller 50 years ago the hero, Ben Hur, is described at the start of a Roman chariot-race as seeing things about him "as through a glass, darkly." This describes the situation of one attempting to peer into the future of the state university, not in any sense of pessimism, but in the sense of the would-be seer, who finds the crystal ball cloudy. Perhaps it is best expressed by quoting a friend who, after reading the 18-year-old report of a distinguished commission on the future of higher education, said the experience ". . . has made me . . . more confident in putting down my thoughts on the future . . . and more relaxed with the prospect that the future may find me equally wrong."[1]

[1] Charles Kidd, "The Evolution of Federal-University Relationships," Montgomery Lecture, University of Nebraska, May 3, 1969.

I have confidence in the future of the state university. It is based on faith—faith that this distinctive institution will survive and progress under the test which J. L. Morrill of the University of Minnesota defined as "the responsibility of the people of a state to their university . . . as great as their faith in the power of inventive intelligence and informed good will, as compelling as the highest aspirations of the human heart."[2]

Yet this confidence, this future, is conditional on the way in which a range of complex policy issues which confront us nationally, in the several states, are resolved.

These involve issues as to the future method of financing higher education which will affect the future of public education as such at all levels; federal policy in higher education; policies and decisions within the several states with respect to the governance, autonomy, allocation of functions and support of higher education; and the ability of universities, specifically state universities, to resolve problems of internal governance.

Let us examine some of the major policy areas in which decisions are to be made:

1. The Future of Public Education

The future of public education at all levels is under severe assault in this country today, from a variety of sources. The "public principle" in higher educa-

[2] James L. Morrill, *The Ongoing State University* (Minneapolis: University of Minnesota Press, 1960), p. 108.

tion is at present the chief target, but there is also a growing drumfire of attack on the public schools. It comes from those who argue that education, or at least higher education, should be paid for by the individual and not society. It comes from those who believe there is a societal responsibility for education, but argue that this should be discharged primarily or exclusively by providing financial support only to or through individuals, or some selected individuals, rather than by the support of institutions.

Two of the principles commonly used today to justify the assault on public education are those of "freedom of choice" and "the necessity of competition."[3]

"Freedom of choice" is an attractive principle. In the private sector, it means that I am free to use my own money to attend the school I wish to attend for whatever morally or educationally good or bad reasons. Its corollary is that the institution is equally free to accept or reject me, for whatever reasons. When public funds are involved, however, I as a taxpayer am willing to have public funds used to improve freedom of individual choice, but within substantial limitations and in the framework of sound

---

[3] See, for example, Theodore R. Sizer, "The Case for a Free Market," *Saturday Review*, January 11, 1969. Also, Donald A. Erickson, "Private Schools and Educational Reform," *Compact* (Education Commission of the States), February, 1970. The "Educational Reform" referred to involves adoption of the "freedom of choice" plan ruled unconstitutional by the federal courts when adopted by several southern states following the 1954 Supreme Court decision in *Brown v. Board of Education*. Dr. Erickson would "keep the public schools available for pupils who were not welcome elsewhere"!

public policy with respect to the use of tax funds. I do not want the "freedom of choice" principle so to dominate public policy in financing education as to destroy public education. I do not want public money used to pay the seller of services any price it chooses to charge, whether it operates as a profit-making or "nonprofit" institution. And I do not want to see the slogan "freedom of choice" used to bypass the Constitution, or the Civil Rights Act.

It is also argued that "competition" is essential for the improvement of education, and that this "competition" should be provided for the public schools through "freedom of choice" by furnishing funds for individuals to attend a wide variety of schools, under a wide range of sponsors. "Competition" is also an attractive principle, but we can have it in a variety of ways without destroying public education to get it. We can have it, for example, by using the resources of a wide range of private (and public) institutions and agencies to operate public schools, to provide specific services, to conduct a wide range of experimental and innovative programs. But these should be, as many are now in higher education in some areas, by contract or arrangement with a public authority and dependent on willingness to be "public" in terms of accountability, responsibility, compliance with public policies governing the use of public funds.

My impression is that a good deal of the current assault on the principle of public education through "freedom of choice" and competition involves a tortuous process of rationalization and conscience-salving by individuals. They rushed, or encouraged others to rush, to the southern barricades in the heady early days of the civil rights movement, protesting against legally enforced segregation and discrimination in the public schools and elsewhere. But they never really believed in or fought for the public schools at home. Confronted with the problems facing the public schools in the ghettos, embarrassed by the fact that they have long used personal affluence to exercise "freedom of choice" in private schools, and faced with *de facto* segregation in the suburbs and in the ghettos, they have turned to "freedom of choice" and "competition" as a way of "eating their cake and having it too." That is, they can continue to stand firmly for principle in demanding full integration and abolition of all forms of discrimination in the *public schools;* and also in favor of the use of public funds to permit it elsewhere.

Many of the proposals for a radical change in the financing of higher education have come from individuals legitimately concerned for the financial plight and problems of private higher education. Because of the fact that most of our national communications media are published or controlled in the Northeast, an area in which private higher education has high prestige, its spokesmen have had no difficulty in getting their voices heard.

As Fred Harvey Harrington of the University of Wisconsin said in his 1969 presidential address to the National Association of State Universities and Land-Grant Colleges: "It is time to speak out for public higher education"[4]—for all public education. Not negatively. As President J. L. Morrill of Minnesota once observed, "The eggs of higher education are truly in one basket." But there is a need for speaking out affirmatively. The state university as a distinctive societal institution will not survive if the public principle in higher education is gravely eroded, or distinctions between the public and private principle obscured. Nor will the private university, as a distinctive institution. We need to emphasize strongly the fundamental importance of strong institutions which keep educational opportunity open at low cost to the student; which provide education of high quality for young people of a wide range of talents and goals; and which are relatively immune to the pressures on academic freedom and integrity which can and do arise from private interests.

2. Issues of Federal-State University Relationships

The future of the state university is deeply involved in the future of the federal role, or roles, in higher education. Major decisions in federal policy in the next decade will undoubtedly have a major influence on state and private policies in the support of higher education, and may well be determinative. No serious student of the needs of the nation thinks that continuing and substantially increased federal financial

[4] Address delivered at the annual convention of the Association, November 11, 1969. Printed separately by the Association, One DuPont Circle, Washington, D.C., and also available in its *Proceedings,* 82nd Annual Convention, 1969.

involvement in the financing of higher education—in some form—is not essential. Even those who style themselves as vigorous foes of federal involvement are among the most vocal supporters of proposals which would take from the U.S. Treasury, in the form of tuition tax credits, sums far in excess of the total present combined budget of the U.S. Bureau of Higher Education and the National Science Foundation.

Even the strongest advocates of the theory that "the student should pay" for higher education want the federal government to establish a "student loan bank" requiring billions of dollars in capital outlay annually, and the use of the Internal Revenue Service as a collection agency.

Governor Rockefeller of New York, a state which is probably both the wealthiest and which has done the most in taxation of its own residents to provide for pressing societal needs, has used dramatic and convincing statistical evidence to show that New York cannot meet its present and future *commitments already made,* without a large-scale infusion of federal funds, or federal assumption of responsibility in certain areas, or both.[5]

Future federal action can, and will, take a variety of forms. Among those proposed are federal assumption of welfare costs (releasing state funds for other pressing needs); "block grants" of federally collected revenues for general or specific purposes;

[5] Governor Rockefeller's statement of the case for greatly expanded federal assistance to the states was made to the President's cabinet and in a series of addresses during 1969.

tax measures which will encourage the states to adopt progressive rather than regressive forms of taxation. These more or less "indirect" methods of improving the fiscal capacities of the states have important implications for higher education.

There is also certain to be a continuing, large-scale, direct federal involvement. It is primarily with this that my remarks are concerned. As I have observed earlier, federal policy in the past 20 years has involved heavy emphasis on advanced study and research; on aid to or through individuals; on aid—or purchase of services—along categorical, mission-oriented lines. The federal government has also tended to operate "like a foundation"—providing funds for specific purposes, taking little responsibility for their future financing; reversing emphasis and policy as new problems command public attention.

Conspicuously lacking has been a large-scale commitment to support of institutions of higher education as such, in short, to the "public principle" in higher education.

Public concern about rising costs of higher education to students has brought aid to help meet them, but not to keep them from rising. Concern about quality has been expressed in terms of project grants to individual institutions, apparently in the hope that results will spread by osmosis. There is little evidence in federal policy of a belief that most institutions of higher education have considerably more competence, knowledge of deficiencies, desire to improve, than funds to make this possible.

Dissatisfaction with the fragmentation, dispersion, and lack of continuity in federal involvement has resulted in widespread demand for improvement and change. Study commissions, task forces, advisers on "priorities" have multiplied, reported, gone home, been succeeded by others.

Considerable support has arisen recently for creation of a national body of advisers on federal educational policy, at the highest levels of government. The national interest in education is so great, it is argued, that coherent policies should be formulated by our best and wisest talent, working on a continuing basis, devising both general and specific policies to meet "national" needs.

Such proposals both attract and frighten me. I feel about them as a young man might who sees a beautiful girl beckoning him—from the other side of a lake covered with thin ice.

Who can be against use of our best minds in planning for higher education—or against beautiful girls? But the ice may break, or the girl may have been merely powdering her nose. And the problem with high centralization in policy-making is that the best and wisest men may be unanimously wrong. The effect of a grossly mistaken policy put into effect nationally is apt to do great damage nationwide, just as a wise policy may do great good.

My belief is that we should of course use the best talent we can find—it is considerably more likely to be right than wrong on balance—but in a context of substantial decentralization of much decision-making to state and other authorities responsible for higher education, and individual public and private institutions.

Most of the present types of federal programs, particularly those involving research, advanced graduate and professional education, and aid to disadvantaged individuals, should be continued and expanded, although subject to modification and improvement. But if the major, and needed, new expansion of federal involvement, particularly at the undergraduate or "collegiate" level, is confined to aid channeled to or through individual students, we will reach the point at which a substantial majority of all students will be directly dependent on one or more federal programs for college attendance. By the same token, the institutions they attend will also be heavily dependent for support both on federal policies and on students.

Diversity and variety of sources and methods of support are essential to diversity, variety, autonomy, freedom, in higher education. The states and private sources should continue to play a major role in the support of higher education, and in the determination of broad policies affecting it. The charge is often made that state government is less responsive to societal needs, less "responsible" than the federal government. The record of the past quarter-century furnishes some substance to this charge, particularly since the cry of "state's rights" has all too often been associated with resistance to the exercise of human rights. But this has not always been so, and may not continue to be so. Indeed there is some basis for the assertion that within the past two years the record of the states in higher education—with some exceptions—has been better than that of the federal government. Unless substantial reforms are accomplished in Congress and a clear commitment to some reasonable priority for higher education emerges within the administration, this may continue to be so for some time.

In any event I would like to see future federal involvement in higher education established within a context, or framework, or set of agreed-on principles.

One is that the federal government should pay the full cost of services it "buys," programs it promotes, as clearly a matter of specific national policy and interest. A good deal of what is usually described as federal "aid" to higher education in fact involves subsidy of "federal" programs by colleges and universities.

A second is that federal involvement include a substantial but not preponderant supportive role for colleges and universities as such. The chief responsibility for decision-making—within broad requirements as to policy, purpose, accountability—would be left with those nonfederal public and private bodies which have historically exercised it. This kind of direct institutional support should encourage, rather than discourage, state and private support, and preservation of the public and private "principle" in education.

Areas in which it was agreed that the federal government should have primary responsibility for public financing should be identified. One of these might, for example, be the reduction or elimination of interstate fiscal barriers to the migration of students. A report on the financing of higher education in Canada of a few years ago (1) found that the migration of students between provinces and the enrollment of significant numbers of foreign students in Canadian universities are educationally and culturally desirable, (2) recommended that distinctions between resident and nonresident fees be eliminated, and (3) held that elimination of such barriers was a national rather than a provincial responsibility, and recommended that the federal government, by negotiation with each province, pay on behalf of nonresident students the difference between the "resident" fee and the actual cost of instruction.[6]

Other areas of primary federal fiscal responsibility would of course include certain aspects of international educational programs or technical and cultural cooperation, many areas of research and graduate and professional training, etc.

Having established a general policy framework, I would then charge any "National Council of Educational Advisers" or any other federally sponsored study group with the responsibility of including in its reports an explicit evaluation and defense of its proposals in terms of this policy framework.

Another major responsibility of a National Advisory Council on Education would be that of in-

[6] *Financing Higher Education in Canada: The Report of the Commission on Financing Higher Education to the Association of Canadian Universities and Colleges* (Toronto: University of Toronto Press, 1965).

terpreting education to the public, on a continuous basis.

Whatever the feasibility of the above specific proposals, we need some arrangement to assure that commissions on the future of higher education and study groups concerned with particular pressing problems *concern themselves with the future of higher education*. It should not be viewed, as is too often the case, as a department store—or corner grocery—in which the federal government can buy needed services, or loan or give money to individuals to shop for whatever is on sale.

Study groups in higher education tend to concern themselves with particular and immediate pressing problems, but *not* with the future of higher education. In their proper concern for the disadvantaged student or the superior student, the plight of the cities or rural areas, health, new sources of income, they neglect the institutions on whose "health, education, and welfare" so much of our society's future "health, education, and welfare" depend.

There is, for example, no unit within the U.S. Office of Education or its Bureau of Higher Education whose explicit concern is with what is happening to colleges and universities as such. There are units concerned with student financial aid, graduate programs, language programs, libraries, facilities, equipment, etc. The result of this is that initiatives for new or expanded programs tend to be in terms of supplementing or expanding existing programs, without examination of their impact on higher education, as such, or indeed of the societal implications of continuing exclusive reliance on present types of programs. If we continue to emphasize borrowing, for example, as the appropriate means of financing higher education, future marriage ceremonies of college graduates may have to include the phrase "with all my college debts I thee endow."

3. Intrastate Relationships: Governance, Coordination, Planning

A third area of fundamental future importance is what for want of a better term I shall call "Intrastate Relationships."

It involves questions of coordination and planning, assignment of institutional functions, cooperation, of place and primacy in the educational hierarchy, quality, identity, autonomy, prestige, political and bureaucratic interference—to name a few.

I shall back into the topic by quoting from a talk by State Senator Robert Graham of Florida, an able and intelligent legislator with a record of interest in higher education, to the 1969 annual meeting of the Association of Executive Officers of Statewide Boards of Higher Education.

Mr. Graham said in part, and I quote: "Theoretically, state boards of higher education are designed to be an interface between the academic and the political community. In fact, from the point of view of the statehouse, the coordinating board is often seen as an institutional lobbyist for the various universities and colleges. This is an unfortunate perspective because it prohibits the emergence of a natural and necessary coalition between state politicians, specifically state legislators, and state coordinating boards. It is a coalition forged of a common history, a common objective, we might even say a common enemy, and the common necessity of confronting difficult policy issues which cannot long be unattended."[7]

Mr. Graham also emphasized the "impending confrontation" implicit in the prospective leveling off of enrollments in higher education, the multiplication of institutional graduate programs in the face of projections of oversupply of traditionally trained Ph.D.'s in certain areas, the "backlash" against campus confrontations, and public demand for greater emphasis on the quality of undergraduate education. He suggested to coordinating boards that in allocating new graduate programs they should avoid the "twin traps of nomenclature and history." The name "university," he said, is now so widely used that it is meaningless as a distinctive institutional identification. As to history, he suggests that those institutions which have in fact historically been established and developed as truly state *universities* "are in danger of isolation from the current trend which emphasizes education for change through involvement." Shifts in political power to urban areas and in educational philosophy might "happily converge," he suggests, if standards for establishment and expansion of graduate programs are applied not in terms of current status but "of where in the state

[7] D. Robert Graham, "Politics and Higher Education Coordination." Occasional Paper No. 2, Education Commission of the States, Denver, Colorado, December, 1969. Address to the Association of Executive Officers of Statewide Boards of Higher Education, Miami, Florida, July 31, 1969.

system the program has the greatest opportunity to achieve distinction."

Senator Graham's remarks pose many of the problems of intrastate and interinstitutional relationships as they affect the state university today.

The forces which have brought about creation of agencies charged with responsibility for planning, coordination, assignment of function in higher education in each state are here to stay. What are their implications for the future of the state university? And of other recent trends and developments?

Problems, traditions, resources, leadership—all differ among the states, and widely differing outcomes may be expected.

A. THE UNIVERSITY IN AN URBAN SOCIETY

It is clear that no single institution or single campus of a multicampus institution can in the future, in most states, "be all things in higher education to all people." Difficult choices must be made. Mr. Graham has indicated that the future major development of the state university "as University" should be in the major urban areas. Herman B Wells, former president of Indiana University, put it somewhat differently. Mr. Wells said that "the state university must turn from a primarily agrarian orientation in its outreach to an urban orientation," appropriate to an urbanized society.[8]

[8] Herman B Wells, "The Growth and Transformation of State Universities in the United States since World War II: The Magnitude and Complexities of the Challenge." Address given at a Conference on the Task of Universities in a Changing World, University of Notre Dame, April 17, 1969.

I would put it differently from either Mr. Graham or Mr. Wells. Of course the state university must be "urban-oriented" in the sense of being concerned with solution of the problems of the great metropolitan areas. Of course the educational needs of young people living in the cities must be served by the expansion of existing institutions and establishment of new institutions, and these will have special opportunities, responsibilities, for developing programs serving their immediate communities. The University of Illinois recognized this in the establishment of its Chicago Circle campus. Indeed, with perhaps three exceptions, there is a major campus of a state university in every major metropolitan area of the country today.

But, as Mr. Henry observed in an address at Wayne State University in Detroit in 1969, "good ideas are not to be evaluated on the basis of geography."[9] All state universities, wherever located, have substantial contributions to make in providing the expertise and the educational services needed for the solution of urban problems. There is also the point which David Riesman once emphasized that the commuting student frequently faces special and severe problems of adjustment as between new ideas and values to which he is exposed on campus, and those held in the home to which he returns nightly. Getting away from home is educationally important to many students.

With regard to Mr. Wells's point that the state

[9] David D. Henry, "The Urban University and Urban Society." Address at the Centennial Convocation, Wayne State University, June 18, 1969.

university must change from an "agrarian" orientation to an "urban" orientation, my difference may be more semantic than substantive. Clearly, in my opinion, the state university must continue to be concerned with the problems and needs of "agriculture" and those engaged in it and dependent on it, which includes all of us. But beyond this it must—if we are ever to solve the problems of the great metropolitan areas—concern itself with the problems of the nonmetropolitan areas and people of the country —those who neither live in the great cities nor are directly engaged in agriculture—as well as those of the great cities.

The most pressing problems of Washington, D.C., and of New York, Chicago, and other great cities originated with the mass migration of refugees from rural areas and small towns who found the door to opportunity closed by an agrarian revolution which made them, as the English say, "redundant," and by a technical-industrial revolution, from which they were barred in large part by lack of education and discrimination. They came to the cities seeking jobs, better schools, housing, treatment, a better life. You know the results. Yet there are still twice as many people, in absolute numbers, below the "poverty line" of income in the nonmetropolitan areas of the country as there are in the cities.

Our hope of both checking and reversing the deterioration of the cities lies heavily in providing better educational opportunities, employment opportunities, recreational and cultural opportunities elsewhere, and thus slowing down and perhaps checking migration into cities from areas where these opportunities do not now exist. In this sense, the U.S. Department of Agriculture may currently be doing more to help solve the "urban problem" than the cabinet agencies officially charged with this responsibility.[10]

My point is that the future of the state university should be thought of as "people-oriented" and "knowledge-oriented" rather than "urban" or "rurally" oriented. There has been some talk, in recent years, of establishing "urban grant" universities—a catchy phrase based on a fallacy. The land-grant universities were not given land to "serve" rural areas or "the wide-open spaces" as contrasted to the cities. They were endowed by the sale of land to serve the people, wherever they lived, and regardless of the locations at which formal instruction of undergraduates was carried on. Since the state university cannot do "all things for all people" it must make choices in terms of its resources and capabilities, in terms of the things it can do—but not in terms of the people its responsibility it is to serve. For example, the University of California many years ago recognized the need for locally available post–high school education, and took leadership in establishing a separate statewide system of community colleges. The University of Kentucky, seeing the same need, established a statewide system of community colleges as part of the University. The university in each case recognized the need and took

[10] I refer to the great emphasis of the Department of Agriculture under Secretary Clifford Hardin and his predecessor, Secretary Orville Freeman, on improving conditions of life in rural areas.

leadership, but made different choices as to its continuing role.

Let us touch on some other problems of an internal nature within the states.

B. HIGHER EDUCATION AND POLITICS

In some states there is evidence of "repoliticalization" of public higher education. In a few states, executive officers or chairmen of statewide boards are beginning to appear in governors' cabinets, with at least the implication that higher education is an administrative department of state government, with direct responsibility to the governor. In others, where elective state administrative and legislative office automatically carries voting membership on university boards of trustees, the inherent contradictions and dangers involved in this dual role are in some cases being manifest. Over a period of many years this was not apparent. Issues in higher education were not a matter of political controversy, and state officials who also served as trustees were generally supportive of university needs and interests in both roles. In the present era of tight budgets and highly competitive claims on resources, of campus confrontations and tensions, some political figures have yielded to the temptation to "run against" the university, a temptation increased when the rival candidate is a member of the university's trustees, and therefore "responsible" for its governance and appraisal of its financial needs. Thus partisan political issues and candidacies have—fortunately in only a few instances—been brought to the fore in consideration of university needs and policies. It is highly desirable, in my opinion, that the properly nonpolitical role of university trustees, and that of the necessarily political role and responsibility of high administrative and legislative officials, be separated—for the good of both.

C. TRENDS IN COORDINATION

Although the trend in state coordination of higher education was for some years to leave existing governing boards "in place" and superimpose upon them a "coordinating" board with varying powers, a recent tendency in states with limited resources has been to create new "single boards" with both policy and operating authority over all public higher education, headed by a "chief executive officer" with wide fiscal, administrative, and representational authority. In at least two states, a high percentage of the top fiscal and administrative staff of the state university has been translated to the staff of the new "state system" or "state university." (This has caused critics to question the necessity of maintaining highly qualified administrative staffs on the various campuses. As one critic wrote, "Should we not on the various campuses replace presidents with administrative deans; chief fiscal officers with bookkeepers and accountants, and so on?") [11]

This leads me to observe that there is a question as to whether or not, in some states, there will continue to be an identifiable institution—single or multi-

---

[11] Clipping from "Letters to the Editor" in a Fairmont, W. Va., newspaper.

campus—with the distinctive characteristics of "the state university" as we know it, as the "capstone" of the state's educational system. There is a possibility that functions, programs, responsibilities, will be so dispersed as to arrive at a "common level" among the various institutions of the state. I avoid the terms "common level of mediocrity" or "absence of high quality" because these involve prestige, elitism, caste. And herein lies part of the problem. We need a new prestige system, or multiple-prestige system, in American higher education. Institutions should have prestige, be recognized, esteemed, for the quality of their work in terms of defined function. California Institute of Technology is certainly an institution of high national prestige and quality in terms of function. But if the standard be the function of providing large numbers of competent teachers for the public schools, several institutions outrank Cal Tech in quality, and should have a high place on the prestige totem pole—or poles. A prominent California legislator recently proposed placing all public post–high school education under a single board, with administrative decentralization along regional lines, and calling the whole structure "The University of California."[12] While this specific proposal would, in my opinion, raise much more serious problems than it would solve, there is an element of perceptiveness in the proposal to solve the problem of prestige and nomenclature by calling all post–high

[12] From the report of a legislative council study group given wide circulation by Jesse Unruh. Mr. Unruh was speaker of the lower house of the California legislature at the time the study was initiated.

school education "The University of California." A rose by another name may, as Shakespeare suggests, "smell as sweet," but it is unlikely that rose-fanciers will ever be brought to think so.

The question for the future is: will it find, within each state, an institution which is distinctive in terms of the mission of exemplifying the highest quality in advanced graduate and professional education, in research on the frontiers of knowledge, and comprehensiveness in terms of student body, programs, and statewide responsibility? Will such a university, and other higher institutions in each state, have the necessary autonomy, integrity, freedom from political interference and bureaucratic controls—and at the same time function as part of a planned, rationally coordinated, efficient system of higher education?

I think this will generally prove to be true, though there will be lapses, setbacks, discouraging countertrends, and shifts in role and function of institutions in some states. My long-run optimism is based on the fact that in every state in which a distinctive state university did not exist—and there were some such until recent years—it has been found necessary and desirable to create one. In some states it may be that the centripetal forces of political and educational regionalism, the tempting but destructive urge to involve higher education in partisan politics, will prevail for a time. If so, the quality of all higher education will suffer, and the distinctive and comprehensive role of the state university may be destroyed. Even so, in the longer run it will again be found that it is bad politics as well as bad education to play partisan politics with higher education; that freedom from centralized bureaucratic and political control is the essential ingredient of true efficiency in higher education; and that a truly comprehensive state university is an essential component of a public higher education system of high quality.

My belief is that in most states it will not be necessary for Phoenix to rise from the ashes, however. Wise resolution of the problems of intrastate relationships will take a dedication by political leaders, concerned citizens, above all by educational leaders, to the proposition that they must all work together in the great common interest of providing the best possible educational service to the people. Legislators, coordinating boards, governors, individual institutions are not, must not be, aligned one way or another as "common enemies"—to use Mr. Graham's phrase. They all exist to serve society through education.

A fallacious assumption underlying some of the destructive types of competition sometimes evident in higher education is that there is a limited "pot" or "pie" of resources available, and that each institution, each unit of an institution, each area of a state, must not only compete for its "share" but at the expense of others. Of course there are limitations on resources, but the basic limitation on the resources the American people are potentially willing and easily able to put into education, including higher education, is far from being reached. They must be convinced, however, that these are being expended wisely for educationally justifiable purposes, and not for enhancement of the prestige of particular institutions, or the economic benefit of a particular community. In a sense, the problem reminds me of a story about a state university in which a particular college rose to great national distinction in its field, under the administration of a certain dean. I asked a colleague the secret of his success. The reply was, "Dean X always took a great interest in the development of the university as a whole. He felt he could not have the kind of college he wanted to have, in a university which was not strong in all its components. He frequently offered to delay major developments in his own field, to give immediate priority to other colleges. As a result, he had the united support of all of us for anything he felt was essential in his field. We knew it was."[13]

This is the spirit we need, in intrastate relationships—working together for the improvement of the whole. The state university must supply leadership in developing it. It must be prepared to share some traditional functions, perhaps give up direct responsibility for some entirely—its role changing from direct responsibility to providing trained leadership, or involvement only to the extent necessary for experimentation and innovation. But the state university cannot do it alone. The state university as traditional standard-setter is in a particularly exposed and vulnerable position. It may be attacked for being too elitist if it sets high admissions standards, and for wasting the taxpayer's money by

[13] The comment was made about A. A. Potter, long-time dean of engineering at Purdue University.

admitting unqualified students if it makes a genuine attempt to reach the economically and culturally disadvantaged.[14] It cannot begin to meet all the legitimate demands for use of its unique resources. In making hard choices it may create hostility and ill will. It, too, needs the sympathetic understanding and cooperation of others. In intrastate relationships, as in national relationships, educators might well adopt as their motto John Donne's lines: "Ask not for whom the bell tolls: It tolls for thee."

4. University Governance

Universities all over the country are reexamining the structure and rationale of their internal governance. In the university, as in the nation, to quote President Homer D. Babbidge of the University of Connecticut: "We are concerned with governing a free society, knowing that the freer it is, the more difficult it will be to govern, and knowing, too, that if it cannot be governed, it cannot be free."[15]

Governance, the exercise of authority, derives from two sources—voluntarily given assent, a "consensus of legitimacy"; and from power. The current crisis in authority is based on the fact that a significant fraction of our people—particularly among minority groups and the young—believes that established authority is illegitimate, is not representing their

---

[14] See note 5, Chapter II, above. See also John Egerton, *State Universities and Black Americans* (Atlanta: Southern Education Foundation, 1969).

[15] Homer D. Babbidge, "Some Thoughts on the University Presidency." Address to the Yale Alumni Board, Oct. 31, 1969.

interests. Some are committed to the destruction of established authority, and particularly of the university as providing the new leadership for established authority. Others seek extensive change and reform, but preferably without chaos and violence, as a means of establishing a new consensus of governance based on respect. University governance through arbitrary exercise of power is, of course, incompatible with preservation of the freedom essential to a university.[16]

This has been recognized in practice by trustees through delegation of power to administrators and faculty, by administrators through delegation to faculty and students.

As Mr. Babbidge commented: "Arbitrary authority is long gone, and the university president finds himself relying increasingly on his powers of persuasion." Yet persuasion and mediation are not enough, particularly in these days of tension and confrontation. At times the university must act, or face disintegration and chaos. The president is the focal point. As administrator, he has responsibility for the implementation of policies fixed by the trustees and by legislative enactments. As president, he must faithfully represent the university community to the trustees, lawmakers, alumni, and a wide range of publics.[17] In the event of campus disruption he cannot, as one private university president said some

[16] Willis Harman, "The Nature of Our Changing Society—Implications for Schools." Paper prepared for the ERIC Clearing House on Educational Administration, Eugene, Oregon, October, 1969. Mr. Harman is director of the Educational Policy Research Center, Stanford University.

[17] Babbidge, *op. cit,* note 15.

time ago to considerable public acclaim, give "five minutes for meditation" followed in 15 minutes by expulsion. Both legally and morally, the university is obligated to give due process, to act equitably. The president must act, knowing both that he is subject to human error and that factors entirely outside his control may determine success or failure. A major problem is how administrators may act, with all feasible consultation, and retain the confidence of the university community essential to continued effectiveness. This confidence must be known to exist.

The president's relationship to the trustees is clear. (Administrators do not have or want tenure.) His relationship to the faculty is much more complex. General votes of confidence or of no confidence are rare indeed. Disapproval of specific actions, by individuals and groups, is frequent and vocal. General confidence may in fact exist, but be so obscured and eroded by criticism over minor issues, failure to speak in support on major issues, that effectiveness is lost. As President James Perkins of Cornell said after his resignation: "I wish the faculty had shown the great confidence and support while I was in office, that they expressed after I had resigned."[18]

The fate of individual university administrators is not the issue. All who enter on administration know the hazards of the post—sometimes described as the most difficult and complex in American public life. But the future capability of universities to attract to administration the kind and quality of men and

[18] As quoted by Mr. Babbidge, *op. cit.*

women needed now as never before is important. Has university administration become too demanding in terms of physical and mental exhaustion, of family sacrifices; too frustrating in terms of perceived accomplishment and recognition? Not yet, in general, but there have been an alarming number of losses in recent years—both in those who have left university administration, and those who know what it involves, and decline to enter it.

Some interesting proposals have been made recently, in the interest of improving the conditions which surround the exercise of authority by university administrators. President Babbidge of Connecticut, musing on the problem, has suggested formulation of a university constitution, which would define in broad terms the role and responsibility of the university, and the responsibilities, powers, duties, and rights of members of the university community: administrators, faculty, students, staff. On ratification, the trustees would assume the role of supreme court of the university. Members of the university community would have the right to bring to that court, directly or on appeal, charges of misfeasance or malfeasance in office, denial of guaranteed rights, interference with the rights of others. If the charges were proven, appropriate penalties would be involved, up to and including removal from office or the university community.[19]

The University of Toronto is trying another approach. It has reconstituted its trustees, previously

[19] This suggestion was made by President Babbidge in a talk to the Fall, 1969, Faculty Convocation of the University of Connecticut.

with responsibility only for the finances of the university, into a much larger group broadly representative of leading citizens of Ontario, alumni, faculty, students, and others. Administrators will in future be chosen by the usual processes for specific terms, subject to reelection at the end of the term, and subject to removal in the interim at any time by a formal vote of no confidence. Provision is made against loss of income in the event of removal from office and for financing an appropriate period of preparation for reentry into full-time teaching or research for those who fail of reelection, or do not choose to run.[20]

Such formal mechanisms for expression or re-expression of confidence may not—should not—be necessary. But the fact they are being suggested, and in some instances tried, is illustrative of the problem, of the necessity for the university community to find ways in which authority can be exercised in terms of support based on respect and mutual confidence, felt and known to exist. The alternative seems all too clear: increasing pressures toward the exercise of arbitrary authority based on power. The proper role of authority is to protect freedom. Power is, in that sense, its ultimate and last resort, its exercise properly conditioned by due process and considerations of equity. The greatest enemies of freedom—freedom for the critics who want drastic change as well as those of other views—are those who in the

[20] From a report of the Commission on University Government, University of Toronto, as summarized in *University Affairs*, the bulletin of the Association of Universities and Colleges of Canada, December, 1969.

name of freedom demand that the university as such engage in only those intellectual activities, actively endorse those and only those philosophies and viewpoints, which they advocate, to the exclusion of others. As Walter Metzger, chief historian of academic freedom, has observed, it is surprising that society—with its instinct for self-preservation and perpetuation—should subsidize freedom of criticism and inquiry. This has happened because courageous faculty members, administrators, students, trustees—with the support in the long run of enlightened politicians and the public—have fought for and protected it. Arbitrary power arbitrarily exercised is antithetical to freedom, and thus to the university. But society will insist that the university be governed, that authority be exercised. That it be governed in the interest of freedom is a challenge worthy of the best minds of any university community.

5. The Future Nature and Functions of the University

There is an extensive current literature, with which I am only marginally familiar, on the appropriate function of the college and the university in our society. Much of it is by scholars concerned with the future of our great private universities, but the debate is pertinent to the future of the state university, since more than half of the two score or more great universities of this country today are public.

One view is exemplified by Dr. Carl Kaysen, director of the Institute for Advanced Study at Princeton, who in an appendix to a recent series of lectures on "The Higher Learning, the Universities, and the Public" suggests that the future of the university may well lie in its abandonment of undergraduate education, and of specialized and professional education not truly compatible with advanced levels of scholarship. The functions of socialization, general education, certification for the "lesser" professions and employment, should be left to a wide range of institutions other than the university. These functions, Dr. Kaysen suggests, are becoming increasingly difficult and expensive to perform. Students' demands for training, certification, "relevance" in the curriculum, and new forms of specialization are the source of an increasing divergency of purpose between students and faculty, whose interests lie primarily in advancing the frontiers of their specialties. Society, he suggests, will clearly support the functions which he suggests the university should abandon. But continued university performance of them will increasingly erode the primary university function. Therefore, Dr. Kaysen suggests, let the university justify its societal support not in terms of the importance of science and scholarship as such—which he feels is not politically viable with those who appropriate public funds—but "in terms of their role in advancing training and their indispensability in maintaining the kind of institutions that can both provide advanced and specialized training, and assist society in applying knowledge to social problems." This role for the university having been established,

Dr. Kaysen suggests, other institutions should be discouraged from entering into highly specialized advanced research and education.[21]

Still others suggest that in view of the complexity and cost of advanced research, particularly in the natural sciences, most future advancement of knowledge will necessarily be done by large research establishments, whether called universities or not, providing training essentially only at the postdoctoral level. In either case, if the view that substantial federal financing of advanced research should be largely confined to "national" universities or research centers, essentially divorced from undergraduate education and many areas of specialized education, should prevail, it would have major implications for state universities.

Some time ago Dr. James B. Conant, president emeritus of Harvard, proposed that the "better colleges" and "better universities" cooperate in a plan under which the universities would guarantee

[21] Carl Kaysen, *The Higher Learning, the Universities, and the Public* (Princeton: Princeton University Press, 1969), pp. 75ff. A somewhat similar view was expressed by T. R. McConnell in remarks before the Higher Education Colloquium in Chicago on March 1, 1970. Dr. McConnell foresaw the emergence of a "network of universities which will be nationally and internationally oriented," suggesting that "some private universities have almost reached this stage of evolution" and that "it is now time for some of the most distinguished public universities to follow suit." Such national universities, Dr. McConnell said, should be concerned primarily with research and graduate, professional, and post-doctoral education, but "might admit a limited number of advanced undergraduates strongly oriented to the ethos of a graduate research institution." Such a network of national universities, as Dr. McConnell observed, would have to depend primarily on federal support for both categorical and general purposes. This being the case, the universities involved could hardly be characterized as either "state" or "private"—but as federal universities.

admission to advanced education to graduates of the selected colleges (reserving some places for graduates of other institutions not in the select circle).[22]

Debate over the proper function of the undergraduate college is extensive. One recent writer, Robert Paul Wolff,[23] suggests limitation of undergraduate education to a three-year period without evaluation, grades, or degrees. This would be "a prolonged moment of transition in which the student tests styles of thought and action according to the Socratic dictum that an unexamined life is not worth living." Admission to professional education would be through competitive examination open to those who had or had not attended college, success being followed by a year of intensive preprofessional education. This view of the proper and exclusive function of the college is appealing, but brings the uneasy remembrance that the Greek view of the education suitable for free men was based on the assumption that most men would not be free and would be trained only to do those things essential to the well-being, comfort, and protection of the free. The high unlikelihood that society will support institutions for the sole purpose of enabling large numbers of young people to examine ways and styles of life, however desirable for the many or attractive to the few, reduces Dr. Wolff's argument essentially to an elitist view of what "college education" should be.

[22] As reported in *The New York Times*.
[23] Review by Peter Brooks of Robert Paul Wolff, *The Idea of the University* (Boston: Beacon Press, 1970). Review in *New York Times Book Review*, Jan. 25, 1970, p. 5.

These views as to the role of the university and the college, the future of advanced research, the desirability of concentrating intellectual talent at a relatively few locations, are important to the future of the state university to the degree they win acceptance, but they are not acceptable patterns for the state university, or for most traditional private universities. The state university can forsake its multipurpose and comprehensive character only at the risk of cutting the roots connecting it to a large segment of the society which supports it. As university it must continue to attract those primarily interested in the advancement of knowledge. As "people's college" it must provide a place for those interested in "testing styles of thought" without abandoning the much larger group whose goal is "a liberal and practical education for the several pursuits and professions of life."

Fiscal and other limitations may push it toward becoming an elitist institution on academic-intellectual lines as suggested by Dr. Conant, but there is little evidence of justification for this on educational grounds. The extensive studies of Dr. Alexander Astin have yet to discover any marked relationship between high selectivity of students and educational "impact." Highly selective institutions, like highly selective social clubs, may be valuable in terms of whom you get to know—but not necessarily in terms of the intellectual development of the students during the undergraduate years.[24]

[24] A report of Dr. Astin's findings appeared in *Science* for August, 1968, pp. 661ff. See also his "Productivity of Undergraduate Institutions," *Science*, April 13, 1962.

Disturbing questions are being raised in the area of criteria of selection. It has long been well known that factors other than grades and test scores, such as motivation, are highly important to academic success. Preliminary research by the American College Testing Program in a new area indicates little correlation between criteria which attempt to measure creativity, leadership, and other qualities generally considered socially desirable, and those designed to predict academic success.[25] At the University of Iowa, a study of three consecutive graduating classes some years after graduation indicates a negative correlation between activity in community affairs and high grades, and a positive correlation between merely passing grades and future community activity.[26] The question is: What are we educating for? If we must be selective, should it be wholly on the basis of one set of desirable criteria—to the exclusion of others? Many a university is troubled by the fact that some of its graduates of great later distinction in public life could not now be admitted.

The state university cannot solve difficult educational problems by ignoring them, or abandoning its responsibilities to others. Its responsibility to society is inescapable. It cannot build an ivory tower and move into it, but its "house of many mansions" should certainly include the ivory tower.

Those concerned with educational policy must

[25] From various research reports of the American College Testing Program, Iowa City, Iowa.
[26] *The University of Iowa Spectator*, Vol. 3, No. 2, November, 1969. Activities and college grade averages of classes of 1949, 1955, and 1960 were analyzed by John W. Lewis.

make difficult choices, however. An oversupply of those with graduate training through the traditional research doctorate, in many fields, is now developing. Are we to have large numbers of highly educated people who are unemployable in terms of their specialties? Certainly careful examination of proposals for establishing graduate programs in those fields in institutions in which they do not now exist, or expansion where they do, is called for. Yet while there may be a prospect of excess supply over demand for individuals educated in certain ways in certain fields, nothing is more certain than that the general demand for men and women with advanced and specialized education will be substantially in excess of the numbers available. As Vice-President Eldon Johnson of the University of Illinois said following the September, 1969, Allerton House conference on planning for the coming decade, there is an increasing demand for "delivery"—for assistance in problem-solving, bringing research into action, in tasks involving extra-disciplinary as well as multi-disciplinary resources.[27] Obviously the state university must be selective in its response, must continue to emphasize knowledge-centered education. Yet new degrees and new types of reward systems for faculty are needed which, as Dr. Johnson commented, are neither "bibliographically centered" nor represent compensation for "mere moral indignation or frenetic activity."[28] Some progress has been made in

[27] *Faculty Letter,* Office of the President, University of Illinois, No. 183, Oct. 10, 1969.
[28] *Ibid.*

developing such systems for excellence in instruction, but not extensively with respect to public service. New methods of student participation must be worked out. At the University of Utah, for example, teaching assistants and other graduate students involved in teaching have recently been extensively involved in seminars on problems of teaching, and in criticism of their own teaching effectiveness and that of their departments generally. The spirit has been one of cooperation for mutual improvement. Preliminary results indicate both improved morale and teaching effectiveness for the students, and a stimulation of interest in teaching effectiveness by tenured staff members.[29]

Much of the responsibility for enabling individuals to find rewarding careers in a society of new demands and changing technologies must, of course, be done through continuing and continuous education.

Curricula in many professional fields show a distinct trend away from high emphasis on specific knowledge and skills which may soon become obsolete, with anticipation of multiple opportunities for "professional refreshment" after graduation. Yet society will continue to demand considerable professional and technical competence from recent graduates. Leaders in industry and business have long stressed a preference for those broadly educated in the liberal arts. Yet employment practices indicate a strong preference for graduates in the technical and professional schools, for whom later on provision is

[29] News release from the University of Utah, Salt Lake City, October, 1969.

made for extensive exposure to the liberal arts and social sciences.

There are many other questions. Undergraduate education in British and some continental universities is highly specialized, under the assumption that formal liberal education has been accomplished in the secondary school, or will be accomplished in the extra-curriculum or after graduation. The American tradition has been to require at least a minimum of liberal or general education in the undergraduate years, with professional and specialized education slowly being extended into the fifth and sixth years, or after the baccalaureate degree. Yet a current criticism of many of our best-known undergraduate liberal arts colleges is that they have increasingly been dedicated to undergraduate specialization in a field of future graduate specialization.

Must we continue to prolong the period of formal education—some of it the result of pressures to keep young people off the employment market? Considerable progress has been made in many universities through opportunities for credit by examination, or combined credit toward both the high school diploma and college graduation. I see no early prospect for, or desirability in, general abandonment of some form of credit-certification or continuing assessment of the quality of work done in the undergraduate college, or for leaving all to one great comprehensive examination, so far as those formally involved in resident instruction are concerned. Indeed the perpetual student, always supposedly preparing for the degree examination, is one of the curses of many universities abroad. Universities are increasingly willing and able to respond to the needs of the serious student who wants and can benefit from maximum flexibility in educational arrangements. Much of the criticism of their "inflexibility" comes from those either without serious purpose, or with serious purposes other than those related to university education.

6. The New Technologies in Education

That I have not earlier referred to the new technologies as related to education is not because of their lack of great importance. Education has been extensively criticized on the ground that it has not sufficiently used technology to reduce unit costs of instruction, the most common comparison being with the increased "productivity" of industry through mass production. Education, of course, is a matter of individual development, not mass production. It has been amply demonstrated that the effectiveness of education in certain areas is substantially improved by use of instructional television, so-called "teaching machines," etc., but usually at increased rather than reduced dollar cost.

The PLATO program at the University of Illinois, initiated in 1959, has shown the possibilities of greatly increased flexibility and effectiveness in instruction through computer-based education (PLATO III). In the next step (PLATO IV) Drs. Alpert and Bitzer see the prospect of use of computer-based instruction at capital and operating costs well within the capacity of a wide range of educational institutions, and with the promise of providing a substantial increase in instructional capacity (up to 20 per cent) at a cost about one-fourth of that of similar expansion through traditional methods. Furthermore, technology would here be used greatly to increase *individualized instruction,* to permit students to learn at their own speed in the light of their own needs, and to permit much more faculty-student interaction in small seminars. Again, since substantial capital investment and changes in traditional methods are involved, too much should not be expected too soon—but the implications are exciting for the future.[30] The process of careful and cooperative research and development over a period of years exemplifies the central role of the university in the service of society.

7. The Future of the State University: The Task Ahead

The future of the state university as a distinctive institution in American society, with the degree of autonomy, freedom, and public support this will require, depends on the one hand on its ability to anticipate, accommodate, and "manage" growth and transformation. On the other it depends on the extent to which it is able to communicate to its many publics an understanding of the central importance

[30] D. Alpert and D. Bitzer, "Advances in Computer-Based Education: A progress report on the PLATO program." Article prepared for publication in *Science,* copy made available in advance of publication.

of the university in the life of the state and nation. It must do the first in order to merit support, to "deserve" to survive, as a distinctive institution. It must do the latter to gain the support needed to make necessary changes, initiate needed new programs, attract individuals of high competence to its staff.

This twin task will require an internal and external involvement of staff and student resources and talents much greater than exists now. Most universities have at least made a beginning on institutional self-study and analysis, and on the study of the university as an institution. This has been done through establishment of Offices of Institutional Analysis and Research, Centers for the Study of Higher Education, studies of the learning process. On the "external" side, some progress has been made. The formal function of "University Relations" is no longer considered adequately discharged by the availability of a news service and information office. It is much more complex than that.

But much more needs to be done in both areas. A much wider range of university resources must become involved, formally by the university and voluntarily on the initiative of members of the faculty and student body, out of the realization that they have a responsibility for making an affirmative contribution to discussion and action involving the future of higher education.

I am emphatically not suggesting that members of the university community abandon their scholarly and critical faculties and engage in a propagandistic effort on behalf of the university externally, or adopt a laissez-faire attitude internally. My faith in the state university as a distinctive institution is such that I believe it will "stand up" under scholarly and critical examination, and make necessary and needed adaptions. But it needs much more of such involvement than it is getting from its own community. Let me give a few examples:

Historians have grossly neglected both the history of the state university as an institution and the impact of its development on that of our society; on major and in my view constructive developments in state, national, and international life.[31]

Much has been written about the economics of higher education in recent months, most of it by economists. With few exceptions, and they are few indeed, most of it would not withstand serious scholarly and critical examination. I am not an economist or an expert in the language of statistics, but I say this flatly both because of the reaction of most distinguished and able economists whom I have asked to comment on a good deal of it and because, armed only with some familiarity with fiscal issues in higher education and a knowledge of simple arithmetic, I can recognize glaring errors in methodology in papers now widely quoted by political decision-makers as authoritative. The need for interdisciplinary involvement in studies which result in fiscal policy recommendations is abundantly clear.

[31] See, for example, the comments of Dr. Louis G. Geiger, professor of history, Colorado College, as reported in the *Newsletter* of the History of Education Society, Vol. I, Issue 3, May, 1969.

For those in political science and public administration, the multiple problems associated with the relationship of the university to the state and national government, and those of internal governance, involve issues of great societal and scholarly importance. The one really significant professional contribution in this field was made by two faculty members of the Johns Hopkins University some years ago, in a study of state government and the university. It was published in a book called *The Campus and the State* and the findings and recommendations in a report called *The Efficiency of Freedom*.[32] They are of great and continuing relevance. If either is known to or cited by faculty members professionally consulted in advising on university relationships with government, I have seen no evidence of it.

Internally, the schools and colleges of law have in some instances made significant contributions in the area of internal university governance and the responsibilities of civil and university authorities in their respective, and sometimes overlapping, areas of jurisdiction. Elsewhere their concern has been sporadic and related to immediate issues rather than examination in depth.

Student organizations might well concern themselves with some of the basic issues of national policy in higher education whose resolution, for good or ill, will profoundly affect them and their successors for

---

[32] *The Efficiency of Freedom: Report of the Committee on Government and Higher Education* (Baltimore: The Johns Hopkins Press, 1959), and Malcolm Moos and Francis E. Rourke, *The Campus and the State* (Baltimore: The Johns Hopkins Press, 1959).

years to come. The capacity of universities to make needed changes, to give attention to pressing social problems, even to deal justly and equitably with issues involving alleged violation of university regulations, is directly conditioned by resources available, and conditions attached to the receipt of funds in federal and state laws and regulations.

These are but a few examples. There are many others.

The future of our educational system generally, of higher education and the state university specifically, will depend on priorities attached to it by the people of this country nationally and in the several states. Other urgent demands on resources are competitive with those of education, and within education there is a great competition, demand, and need for assigning priorities. Yet unless the central importance of education at all levels is fully appreciated, the prospect for solution of our other problems is dim.

Today there is general appreciation of the importance of education in the earliest years to the future development of individuals. It is said that other levels of education must be given low priority, so that much greater attention and resources can be put into what we once characterized as "the preschool years." The public is dissatisfied, and properly so, with the results of programs hastily devised to focus on this area, and those intended specifically to improve education of the economically and culturally disadvantaged in the public schools.

Yet we know of the importance of "preschool" education only through the most careful research and experimentation by those trained at the very highest level. They warned that the conditions under which their results were produced could not be immediately translated on a mass scale. A large-scale "action" program in this area urgently needs the continuing contribution of painstaking research and scholarship, lest the results produce only more frustration and disappointment. In the area of environmental pollution we face danger of response to aroused public opinion by frenetic search for instant miracles, followed by disillusionment. We have specific information about the dangers of air and water pollution, of unchecked soil erosion, of disturbing the "balance of nature," largely due to the work of highly trained scientists and technicians whose warnings went unheeded for many years.

The public concern we must have as a basis for action. A continuance of sound research, investigation, and instruction we must also have if concern is to be translated into *effective* action. Since action must proceed without the development of perfect predictability through research—and indeed is the means by which applied research is tested—we need also to develop a public tolerance for error in education at least remotely comparable to that existing in other areas of public and private endeavor. Education, for example, might be given, say, one per cent of the tolerance accorded to error in the production of military hardware, in estimates of the economic benefit of construction of dams and waterways, in the development of new models of cars, and even in the construction of office buildings for legislators.[33] We should not demand that the garden of education produce fine new specimens of success in bold experimentation and innovation, if we threaten to turn off the water if all the plants fail to bloom in profusion the first season.

We need something of the spirit that caused the Congress to pass and President Lincoln to sign the Land-Grant College Act of 1862 in the midst of the Civil War—faith in the future, faith in our young people, faith in education.

As President David D. Henry of the University of Illinois said in 1961, writing on priorities for education: "Considering the central place of higher education in the health, prosperity, and security of the nation, now is not the time to alter our goals simply because we have more people to serve. . . ." Or, one might add in the light of the situation in 1970, ". . . more problems to solve."

Mr. Henry then observed, quoting John Gardner, that education should be "our national preoccupation, our passion, our endeavor" in order that our schools and colleges be at the heart of the national endeavor and not so often trying to "swim upstream

---

[33] For example, the widely publicized overruns in original cost estimates in production of various weapons for the Department of Defense; the substantial errors based on "consumer research" attending the production of the ill-fated Edsel car by the Ford Motor Company; current controversy over cost-benefit ratios for the Florida Inter-Coastal Waterway as determined by the U.S. Army Corps of Engineers; and extensive overruns on advance cost estimates for construction of the Rayburn House Office Building.

against the interest of a public that thinks everything else more urgent."[34]

We are *not*, as Mr. Henry also observed, held back by "lack of capacity or power. As a people, we can accomplish what we set out to do. Our choice, not our means, can be decisive."

Our choice, not our means, will be decisive as to the future of the state university. In venturing to discuss its future, I have come neither as a prophet of doom nor of salvation. It would be foolish to predict that the future of the state university as a distinctive institution is assured because of either its great contributions of the past or its great potential for the future. It is, to paraphrase President Harrington of Wisconsin, "time to speak out for the state university."

It is time to speak out because, as Jonathan Baldwin Turner of Illinois observed, it represents "the greatest of all interests ever committed to a free state —the interest of properly and worthily educating all the sons of her soil."[35]

[34] David D. Henry, *What Priority for Education?* (Urbana: University of Illinois Press, 1961), pp. 84–85.
[35] Mary Turner Carriel, *The Life of Jonathan Baldwin Turner* (Urbana: University of Illinois Press, 1961), p. 83.

Bibliographical Note

This book is not the result of extensive scholarly research, and the author has compiled no bibliography. However, suggestions as to special sources of both bibliographical and other material may be useful to future scholars.

No comprehensive history of the development of the "state university" in this country exists. Valuable textual and bibliographic material will of course be found in the general histories of higher education such as Rudolph's *The American College and University* and *Higher Education in Transition* by Brubacher and Rudy. Another excellent source is *The Campus and the State* by Moos and Rourke, emphasizing relationships between state government and state universities, and with an extensive bibliography. All the above are cited herein.

The land-grant college movement, integrally involved in the development of a substantial majority of major state universities, has fared somewhat better at the hands of historians. A comprehensive history, Eddy's *Colleges for*

Our Land and Time, was published in 1957. Among other highly important sources are Ross's *Democracy's College,* tracing development of the movement to approximately 1900, and three volumes by Alfred Charles True, all published by the U.S. Government Printing Office and dealing respectively with the development of "Agricultural Education" (1929), "Agricultural Experimentation and Research" (1937), and "Agricultural Extension Work" (1928). Also there is the massive two-volume report of the *Survey of Land-Grant Colleges and Universities,* directed by A. J. Klein for the U.S. Office of Education and published in 1930 by the U.S. Government Printing Office as Bulletin No. 9, 1930, U.S.O.E. The series, "Statistics of Land-Grant Colleges and Universities," covering many decades and perhaps the best source of comparative statistics on any one group of higher institutions in this country, was, unfortunately, "temporarily suspended" following publication of the 1963 annual report, and has not been resumed by the U.S. Office of Education.

Major materials related to the celebration of the Centennial of the Morrill Land-Grant College Act, culminating in 1962, are in the library of the University of Missouri at Columbia.

The University of Connecticut library during 1969 initiated an effort to obtain as complete a collection as possible of histories of individual state and land-grant universities, and other important related materials.

An extensive source of basic materials exists in the files of the National Association of State Universities and Land-Grant Colleges, Suite 710, One DuPont Circle, Washington, D.C. 20024. These include the annual *Proceedings* of that Association, oldest among institutional associations in this country, since 1887; the *Proceedings* of the former National Association of State Universities from its founding in 1895; and an (incomplete) series of *Proceedings* of the Conference of Presidents of Negro Land-Grant Colleges, merged with the N.A.S.U.L.G.C. in 1954. Minutes of the executive committees of the first two named Associations and those of the former State Universities Association (non-land-grant state universities) also are available over a substantial period, together with a considerable volume of duplicated and printed materials.

Two factors make this area particularly attractive to future scholars: (1) the existence of a rich volume of relatively untapped source material and (2) the fact that comparatively little has been published and most of the major published works are now out of print.

R. I. T.

A Note on the Author

Russell I. Thackrey received his B.S. and M.S. degrees from Kansas State University. His 15 years of campus teaching and administration (Kansas State and University of Minnesota) were followed by 23 years on the national scene in Washington, D.C., during which time he received honorary doctoral degrees from several universities. He has served on national advisory boards including President John F. Kennedy's Task Force on Education. He recently retired as executive director (emeritus) of the National Association of State Universities and Land-Grant Colleges. Mr. Thackrey has published many articles in education and political science journals; *The Future of the State University* is his first book.

UNIVERSITY OF ILLINOIS PRESS